THE PALACE OF HOLYROODHOUSE

Official Souvenir Guide

ROYAL COLLECTION PUBLICATIONS

Published by
ROYAL COLLECTION ENTERPRISES LTD
St James's Palace, London SW1A 1JR

For a complete catalogue of current publications, please write to the
address above, or visit our website at www.royalcollection.org.uk

Text by Deborah Clarke
Picture research by Deborah Clarke
© 2009 Royal Collection Enterprises Ltd
Text and reproductions of all items in the Royal Collection
© 2009 HM Queen Elizabeth II

010229/09

ISBN 978 1 905686 01 8

British Library Cataloguing in Publication Data:
A catalogue record of this book is available from the British Library.

Designed by Baseline Arts Ltd, Oxford
Production by Debbie Wayment
Printed and bound by Streamline Press Ltd, Leicester

The unique status of Holyroodhouse as a working royal palace
means that paintings and works of art are sometimes moved at
short notice. Pictures and works of art are also frequently lent
from the Royal Collection to exhibitions all over the world.
The arrangement of objects and paintings may therefore
occasionally vary from that given in this book.

For ticket and booking information please contact:
Ticket Sales and Information Office
Buckingham Palace, London SW1A 1AA

Booking line: +44 (0)20 7766 7300
Group bookings: +44 (0)20 7766 7321
Fax: +44 (0)20 7930 9625
Email: bookinginfo@royalcollection.org.uk
        groupbookings@royalcollection.org.uk
        www.royalcollection.org.uk

Title page: One of the heraldic supporters of the Royal Arms
of James V, in the wall of the palace entrance at Abbey Strand.

All works reproduced are in the Royal Collection, © 2009
HM Queen Elizabeth II unless indicated otherwise below.
Royal Collection Enterprises are grateful for permission to
reproduce the following:

Front cover (main picture) John Freeman; *(right box)* Crown ©
Back cover (top and bottom boxes) Peter Smith; *(middle box)* Empics;
Page 1, 15 (bottom right), 22, 27 (top left), John Freeman; *page 2, 5 (top),
8, 26, 29 (bottom), 30 (both), 32 (all), 33 (both), 35 (both), 36 (both), 37 (both),
39 (both), 40 (both), 41 (right), 42 (all), 45, 46 (all), 47 (top left, top right),
48 (both), 49, 50, 52 (top), 54 (bottom), 55 (bottom left and right), 58, 59, 61
(top right), 62 (bottom right)* Peter Smith; *page 2 (right), page 4 (top left),
28* Getty Images; *page 4 (bottom left)* BCA Films; *page 5 (bottom left),
6 (both), 44, 63 (bottom right)* Empics; *page 5 (bottom right), 61 (bottom),
62 (bottom left), 63 (top and middle), 64 (top and middle)* Peter Packer;
page 7 Crown ©; *page 8 (bottom), 10 (bottom), 14 (bottom)* Scottish
National Portrait Gallery; *page 9 (top), 19 (top)* National Gallery of
Scotland; *page 9 (bottom)* Wildfire Televison/Videotext
Communications Ltd; *page 10 (top)* by permission of the British
Library (Cotton Augustus I.ii.56); *page 12 (bottom), 17, 18 (bottom),
21, 34 (both), 51, 52 (bottom left), 53, 60* Antonia Reeve; *page 14 (top left)*
Bodleian Library, University of Oxford (Gough Maps 39, fol. IV);
page 14 (top right), 34 (bottom) G Newbery; *page 15 (top left)* ©
NTPL/John Bethell; *page 15 (middle right)* the property of the
Incorporation of Wrights & Masons of Edinburgh, in the
collection of the Edinburgh Trades Maiden Fund; *page 41, 43 (all),
54* Simon Morison; *page 56* Tom Scott; *page 57* Reproduced courtesy
of RCAHMS (Scottish Colorfoto Collection)
Inside back cover (top and middle left) Scottish National Portrait Gallery;
(bottom left and 2nd right) Antonia Reeve; *(top right)* G Newbery

Every effort has been made to
contact copyright holders;
any omissions are inadvertent,
and will be corrected in
editions if notification of
the amended credit is sent
to the publisher in writing.

Contents

The Palace of Holyroodhouse

ABOVE: *The Queen and Lord Airlie, Captain-General of the Royal Company of Archers, at a garden party in the palace gardens in 2005.*

ABOVE: *Gordon Ramsay receives his OBE from The Queen at an investiture at the palace in 2006.*

THE PALACE OF HOLYROODHOUSE stands in a spectacular setting at the foot of the Royal Mile in Edinburgh, its walled gardens surrounded by open parkland and overlooked by the dramatic Salisbury Crags and Arthur's Seat, an extinct volcano. It is adjacent to the remains of Holyrood Abbey, one of the finest medieval abbeys in Scotland. Although Holyroodhouse has been a royal residence for over 500 years, the palace has not experienced the continuous royal occupation of the other principal British royal residences, Windsor Castle and Buckingham Palace. Its varied history reflects its differing, often intermittent, use by the monarchy over the centuries.

Today the palace is the official residence of Her Majesty The Queen in Scotland. The Queen is Head of State of the United Kingdom of Great Britain and Northern Ireland, and Head of the Commonwealth. Her Majesty is also Head of State of 16 of the Commonwealth's 53 member countries.

Holyroodhouse is a working royal palace and a centre for national life whenever members of the Royal Family are resident. The Queen is officially in residence at Holyroodhouse once a year, for a week during the summer, at which time she carries out a wide range of official engagements at the palace, in Edinburgh and throughout Scotland. The Queen holds investitures in the Great Gallery for the distribution of honours; audiences are held in the Morning Drawing Room; and a luncheon takes place in the Throne Room on the installation of new Knights to the Order of the Thistle, Scotland's oldest order of chivalry. The Queen and the Duke of Edinburgh also hold a garden party within the palace grounds, to which Scots from all walks of life are invited. Occasionally the palace is used for ceremonial visits by foreign heads of state. President Putin

BELOW: *The Queen, in Thistle Robes, arrives for the Thistle Service at St Giles Cathedral, Edinburgh, 2006.*

ABOVE: *The south side of the palace viewed from Arthur's Seat.*

BELOW: *The palace at night.*

THE ROYAL COMPANY OF ARCHERS

The Royal Company of Archers was founded in 1678 as an archery club. It received its royal charter from Queen Anne in 1704 and was created The King's Bodyguard for Scotland by George IV on his visit in 1822. The Royal Company provides detachments for investitures and for the garden party at Holyroodhouse, and Guards of Honour for the installation of Knights of the Thistle, the opening of the Scottish Parliament and other ceremonial occasions attended by The Queen. Members carry a longbow and wear a distinctive uniform of dark green tunic and trousers, a Balmoral bonnet with the Royal Company's badge and an eagle feather. Archery remains an important aspect of the Royal Company's life and many members participate in the annual competitions, including The Queen's Prize, which takes place in the gardens of the palace in June.

At certain times the Royal Company presents the reigning monarch with a 'Reddendo'. This originally took the form of a pair of barbed arrows resting on a green velvet cushion. During The Queen's reign, a Reddendo has been presented on three occasions, departing from tradition in the presentations made: a diamond and emerald brooch in 1952, an engraved glass vase in 1976 and a gold and enamel pen stand in July 2006.

ABOVE: *The Royal Company of Archers on duty.*

LEFT: *The Queen is presented with a Reddendo by the Royal Company of Archers, 2006.*

THE LORD HIGH COMMISSIONER

The Lord High Commissioner is The Queen's representative at the General Assembly of the Church of Scotland. After the formation of the Scottish Presbyterian Church in 1560, Assemblies took place from time to time, usually in the presence of the sovereign. In 1603, when James VI of Scotland succeeded to the English throne, he appointed a Lord High Commissioner to represent him at the Assembly. In 1834, William IV permitted the Lord High Commissioner to take up residence in the palace during the annual meeting of the General Assembly. Today the Commissioner still carries out these duties on behalf of The Queen, occupying the Palace for one week in May.

Holyrood is a house of many memories. Wars have been plotted, dancing has lasted deep into the night, murder has been done in its chamber.

ROBERT LOUIS STEVENSON
Edinburgh, Picturesque Notes, 1878

RIGHT: *The Queen inspects a Guard of Honour of the Royal Regiment of Scotland at the Ceremony of the Keys on her arrival at the palace, July 2006.*

of Russia was entertained at the palace during his State Visit in 2003. Whenever The Queen is in residence the Royal Standard, rather than the Royal Banner of Scotland, is flown. The Duke of Hamilton (the Hereditary Keeper of the Palace), the Royal Company of Archers, and the High Constables of Holyroodhouse are all on duty during the Royal Visit.

His Royal Highness The Prince Charles, Duke of Rothesay, is resident for one week during the summer, carrying out numerous official engagements. The State Apartments are also used frequently by members of the Royal Family for events in support of charitable organisations of which they are patrons.

The State Apartments, located mainly on the first floor, are furnished with numerous fine paintings and other works of art, many of which have long associations with the palace. Treasures from the Royal Collection can also be seen in the changing exhibitions in The Queen's Gallery, created from two buildings within the Mews and opened in 2002 as part of The Queen's Golden Jubilee celebrations. The Royal Collection is held in trust by The Queen as Sovereign for her successors and the nation. The revenue from admissions to Holyroodhouse is directed to the Royal Collection Trust, a registered charity which exists to preserve the Collection to the highest standards and to make it as accessible as possible to members of the public.

ABOVE: *The symbol of Holyroodhouse:
the stag's head with a cross between its antlers.*

ABOVE: *Portrait of James IV, probably painted in the
late 16th century.*

Historical introduction

THE ORIGINS of the Palace of Holyroodhouse lie in the foundation of an Augustinian abbey in 1128 by David I (r.1124–53), on forested land below the slopes of the old volcanic mound of Arthur's Seat. Medieval legend associates the founding of the abbey with King David's vision of a stag, with a cross or 'rood' between its antlers, which he took to be a sign. The name Holyrood may also derive from the precious relic, a fragment of the True Cross, which had been brought to Scotland by David I's mother, St Margaret. The King dedicated his new religious foundation to the Holy Rood.

The Abbey of Holyrood prospered and, from an early date, contained royal chambers for use by the sovereign. By the time Edinburgh became the capital of Scotland in the 15th century, kings chose to reside at the abbey, surrounded by pleasant gardens and a large park for hunting, rather than at Edinburgh Castle, on its exposed rocky summit. James II (r.1437–60) was born at Holyrood in 1430, and was crowned, married and eventually buried in the abbey. James III (r.1460–88) married Margaret of Denmark there. Although the king and his retinue were initially housed in the abbey's guesthouse, by the second half of the 15th century they occupied specific accommodation. Eventually, the royal lodgings came to eclipse those of the abbey in both size and importance.

The early palace of James IV

IT WAS JAMES IV (r.1488–1513), a frequent visitor, who decided to convert the royal lodgings into a palace. His impending marriage prompted him to provide a suitable residence for his new bride, Margaret Tudor, daughter of Henry VII. The wedding was celebrated in the Abbey Church in August 1503, but the new building works were not completed for another year. Although virtually nothing survives of these early buildings, it appears they were laid out around a quadrangle, occupying a

similar position to the quadrangle of the present palace. Principal rooms, including the royal lodging and the chapel, occupied the first floor. A tower was added on the south side to provide extra accommodation for the sovereign. Excavations in 2006 revealed the outline of this building. Traces are still visible of the gatehouse, built to serve both abbey and palace, situated at the north-west corner of the present Forecourt. Work also began on the palace gardens and in 1507 a loch beside the abbey was drained to provide additional space.

THE MENAGERIE

Many European courts had a collection of exotic beasts. In Scotland the principal royal menagerie was at Holyroodhouse. In 1506 James IV was presented with a lion, and also received gifts of a civet cat and two bears. These animals appear to have been kept within the gardens, where a lion yard and a stone lion house were built in 1512. In 1535–6 an ape was given to James V. The menagerie was maintained throughout the 16th century and included lynx, tigers and gamecocks.

LEFT: *Reconstruction of the abbey and palace as it may have looked in the mid 16th century.*

ABOVE: *The palace as depicted in the so-called English Spy Map of c.1544.*

BELOW: *Portrait of James V, probably painted in the late 16th century.*

The remodelled palace of James V

FURTHER CONSTRUCTION of the palace took place during the reign of James V (r.1513–42). Work began in 1528 on a massive rectangular tower, rounded at the corners, to provide new royal lodgings at the north-west corner of James IV's palace. Designed in traditional Scottish style, the tower's prime function was residential, but it also provided a high degree of security; it was equipped with a drawbridge and probably protected by a moat. This tower is the oldest part of the palace that survives today. An ambitious plan to construct a matching tower in the south-east corner was delayed due to James's premature death, but the scheme was finally implemented by his great-great-grandson, Charles II.

The west front was rebuilt to house additional reception rooms. The elegant design incorporated a double-towered gateway, battlemented parapets, ornamental crestings and large windows with great expanses of glazing. The south side was remodelled and included a new chapel; the old chapel became the Council Chamber. These domestic areas may have been begun in anticipation of James V's marriage in 1537 to Madeleine of Valois, daughter of Francis I, King of France. Madeleine died at the palace only 40 days after arriving in Scotland, but links with France were preserved by James's second marriage in 1538 to Mary of Guise, who was crowned in the abbey. The marriages also initiated major works at his other Scottish residences, Falkland Palace and Stirling Castle.

The King's Wardrobe was at Holyroodhouse, where his tailors and embroiderers were based, along with *tapissiers*, responsible for tapestries and other furnishings, many of which were moved from one residence to another as required by the king.

BELOW: *West front of the palace of James V by James Gordon, c.1649.*

RIGHT: *Bird's eye view of the palace from the south by James Gordon, 1647.*

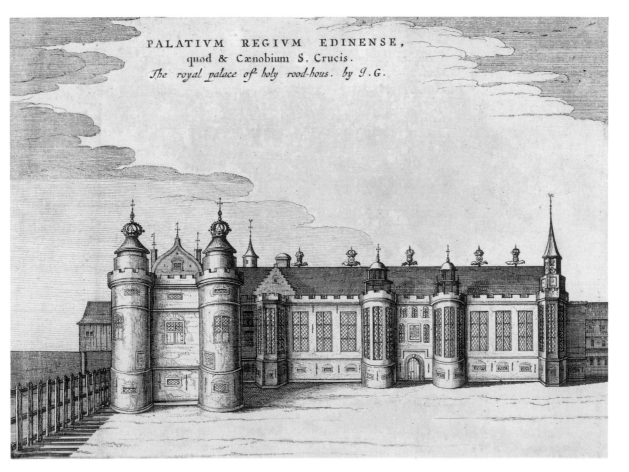

PALATIVM REGIVM EDINENSE,
quod & Cænobium S. Crucis.
The royal palace of holy rood-hous. by J.G.

ABOVE: *British School,* Mary, Queen of Scots, *1603–35*

ABOVE: *Paul van Somer,* James VI and I, *c.1618*

Mary, Queen of Scots at Holyroodhouse

JAMES V'S DAUGHTER MARY (r.1542–67) succeeded to the throne of Scotland on her father's death in 1542, when she was only a few days old. During the 1540s, both the palace and the abbey suffered badly from attacks by English troops during the Rough Wooing, when Henry VIII tried to force the Scots to accept a marriage between his son Prince Edward and the infant Mary. In 1548 Mary was sent away to be brought up at the French court, leaving Scotland in the care of her mother, Mary of Guise. Ten years later Mary married the heir to the French throne. Following the sudden death of King Henry II of France in 1559, Mary's husband succeeded as Francis II, but he died in 1560. The young Queen of Scots returned to Scotland in 1561, a Catholic in a strongly Protestant country. Mary came to live at Holyroodhouse, occupying the Queen's Apartments on the second floor of James V's Tower.

Many of the dramatic events of Mary's short reign took place in the abbey or palace. She married her second husband, Henry, Lord Darnley, in the palace chapel in 1565, and her Italian secretary, David Rizzio, was murdered in her apartments. Her son James was born a few months later and, following Darnley's death in mysterious circumstances, Mary married her third husband, James Hepburn, Earl of Bothwell, in the palace. She was forced to abdicate in favour of her infant son and she fled Scotland. She was kept in captivity in England by Elizabeth I and finally, in 1587, she was executed at Fotheringhay Castle.

The palace under the early Stuarts

MARY'S SON, JAMES VI (r.1567–1625), took up residence in the palace in 1579. Extensive repairs were carried out and the gardens were enlarged and improved. By the time his queen, Anne of Denmark, was crowned in the abbey in 1590, a large court was in residence and the household numbered around 600 people. From 1603, however, when James succeeded to the English throne as James I and the court moved to London, the importance of Holyroodhouse faded. Renovations had to be made prior to the King's return to Edinburgh in 1617, particularly to the chapel and outer areas. External buildings, originally part of the abbey, were absorbed into the palace and ancillary buildings were erected outside the main courtyard and used to house various officials.

The palace and abbey were renovated further in 1633 for the Scottish coronation of James's son, Charles I (r.1625–49). Major repairs and additions were made to the surviving nave of the abbey, where the coronation was to take place. The solemn, anglicised service offended many Scots and the King's ensuing religious inflexibility led to the signing of the National Covenant in Scotland in 1638 and the outbreak of the Civil War in 1639. Turmoil followed the execution of Charles I in 1649 and the Scottish coronation of his son, Charles II, in 1651. The Lord Protector, Oliver Cromwell, travelled north to impose Parliament's authority on Scotland. The palace, occupied as a barracks by Cromwell's troops, was damaged extensively by fire and poorly repaired.

ABOVE: *Daniel Mytens,* Charles I, *1628*

BELOW: *Wenceslaus Hollar's bird's eye view of Edinburgh from the south, with Holyroodhouse on the right, 1670.*

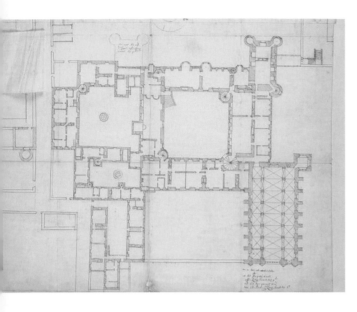

LEFT: *Part of a first floor plan of the palace by John Mylne, 1663.*

ABOVE: *Peter Lely,* Charles II, *c.1670*

The rebuilding of the palace under Charles II

CHARLES II (r.1660–85) was restored to the throne in 1660. Holyroodhouse once again became a royal palace and the regular meeting place of the Scottish Privy Council. A full survey was carried out in 1663 by the King's Master Mason, John Mylne, and in 1670 funds were voted for its repair. Building began in 1671 and the King took a close interest in the work, simplifying the plans to keep costs to a minimum. The work was effectively overseen and directed by the Secretary of State for Scotland, John Maitland, Earl of Lauderdale (1616–82; created 1st Duke of Lauderdale in 1672). The designs were drawn up by the Scottish architect Sir William Bruce, appointed Surveyor General of Royal Works in Scotland in 1671. Robert Mylne, the King's Master Mason from 1668 and nephew of John Mylne, was responsible for the execution of the work.

The successful design of the palace as it is today is due to Bruce's skill in synthesising the new with the old and ensuring a smooth continuity with earlier buildings. The 16th-century north-west tower was balanced with a matching south-west tower, giving a symmetrical appearance to the new entrance façade. The towers were linked by a two-storey front, with a central entrance flanked by giant columns framing the Royal Arms of Scotland, in flat-faced, ashlar masonry. Behind this screen, the existing quadrangular plan was retained and rooms were arranged around

ABOVE: *J. M. Wright,* Sir William Bruce, *1664*

ABOVE: *The Duke and Duchess of Lauderdale by Peter Lely, c.1675*

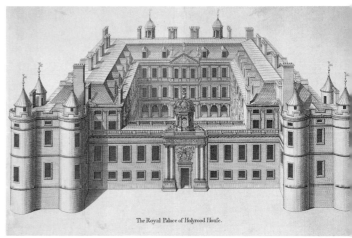

ABOVE: *Elevated view of Holyroodhouse from the west, engraved by Pierre Fourdrinier, c.1750*

ABOVE: *Roderick Chalmers,* The Incorporation of Wrights and Masons at Holyrood, *1720*

ABOVE: *The foundation inscription in the Quadrangle of the palace. In abbreviated form it reads* 'founded by Robert Mylne, Master Mason, July 1671'.

a courtyard with superimposed classical pilasters. On the ground floor, the open, cloister-like quadrangle reflected the palace's monastic origins. Bruce's classical design, combined with the sumptuous baroque interiors overseen by Lauderdale, placed Holyroodhouse in the forefront of fashion. The façades of the quadrangle were the first wholehearted use of the classical orders in Scotland, and were to influence the design of numerous grand houses throughout the country.

A new Royal Apartment for the King was created on the east side, overlooking the planned Privy Garden, while accommodation for his Queen, Catherine of Braganza, was formed from the old Royal Apartment in James V's Tower. A gallery running the length of the north side linked the King's and Queen's Apartments. Both sets of apartments included suites of rooms leading from a Guard Hall, through a Presence Chamber and a Privy Chamber, to an Ante-Chamber and a Bedchamber, the decoration progressively increasing in richness. As with the exterior, the classical orders were used in a hierarchy to denote the rising status of each room as the visitor approached the royal presence. The Council Chamber was created in the new south-west tower. The second-floor rooms provided space for the court when the King was in residence; for the remainder of the time they accommodated the officers of state or hereditary officers of the household. Construction continued apace, and by the end of 1674 the shells of the three main sides of the palace and the new tower were virtually finished. Two years later the west front, which linked the towers, was completed.

ABOVE: *Peter Lely,*
James VII and II
when Duke of York,
c.1665

ABOVE: *The interior of
the Chapel Royal,
showing the furnishings
created for James VII
and II in 1687. Engraving
after Jan Wyck.*

The richly decorated interior of the palace was created by the team of talented craftsmen brought to Scotland by the Duke of Lauderdale. The series of elaborate, high-relief ceilings were by English plasterers John Houlbert and George Dunsterfield, who also worked for Lauderdale and Bruce in their private houses, Thirlestane Castle and Balcaskie. Alexander Eizat, a Dutchman, panelled the rooms in a classical style combined with ornate decoration. Fellow Dutchmen Jacob de Wet and Jan van Santvoort were responsible for the decorative painting and sculptural enrichment of the interiors. Both men worked on other Scottish country houses during this period, including Glamis Castle, the childhood home of Her Majesty Queen Elizabeth The Queen Mother. All these contributions created a striking baroque unity, particularly in the rooms that were completed, such as the King's Bedchamber.

Finally, towards the end of Charles II's reign, de Wet was commissioned by the King to paint a sequence of 110 portraits of Scottish monarchs for the Great Gallery. These portraits not only preserved the likenesses of recent Stuarts, but also, in the royal palace of Scotland, reasserted the Stuart succession to the throne.

The palace under James VII and the later Stuarts

ALTHOUGH CHARLES II and his Queen never stayed at the newly rebuilt Holyroodhouse, his brother James, Duke of York and his wife, Mary of Modena, took up residence in 1679, and again in 1681–2. On the second occasion, the Duke, a Catholic, was sent to Scotland as the Royal Commissioner to Parliament, conveniently escaping anti-Catholic feeling in England at the time. His interest in the palace continued after his succession to the throne in 1685 as James VII of Scotland and II of England (r.1685–89). At this time he ordered the conversion of the Council Chamber in the south-west tower to a Catholic chapel. In 1687 the King issued a royal warrant commanding that the Abbey Church, as Chapel Royal, be converted for Catholic worship and used as the chapel for the revived Order of the Thistle. New altar plate was commissioned and a Jesuit College was established in the precincts of the palace.

Before the Chapel Royal could be completed, the King's fortunes changed. In 1688 his Dutch Protestant son-in-law,

William of Orange, landed in Devon to claim the throne. James was forced to flee to France. On hearing the news of William's arrival in London, a mob in Edinburgh ransacked the abbey and the Jesuit College and destroyed all traces of Catholic worship.

The later Stuarts had little interest in their Scottish residence. The palace was left in the care of the Duke of Hamilton, who took over the Queen's Apartments in James V's Tower and lived there in great luxury. Charles I had appointed the 1st Duke of Hamilton, the premier peer of Scotland, as Hereditary Keeper of the Palace and granted him apartments in Holyroodhouse. The office of Hereditary Keeper is still held by the Dukes of Hamilton.

Following the Act of Union in 1707, which united the kingdoms of Scotland and England, the Scottish Parliament was dissolved and the Council Chamber became redundant. Thereafter the palace provided sumptuous grace-and-favour apartments for members of the Scottish nobility, including the Earl of Breadalbane and the Duke of Argyll.

Prince Charles Edward Stuart at Holyroodhouse

HOLYROODHOUSE briefly came to life once more as a royal palace with a court in residence in 1745. Prince Charles Edward Stuart (1720–88) led the attempt to claim the throne of Great Britain for his father, James Francis Edward, the son of James VII and II. In September 1745 he seized Edinburgh and set up court at the palace. Holyroodhouse became the symbolic residence of the Stuart Prince, known as Bonnie Prince Charlie, in his Scottish capital. The Prince's entry into the palace was recalled later by Lord Elcho, who had accompanied him: 'he mounted his horse and rode through St Anne's yards into Holyroodhouse amidst the cries of 60,000 people, who fill'd the air with their acclamations of joy'.

The Prince occupied the elegant apartments of the Duke of Hamilton, rather than the neglected King's Apartments. It was here that he conducted his official business. He lunched in the palace in public view. The Great Gallery possibly served as a guard chamber during the day, as imagined in Sir Walter Scott's novel *Waverley*:

ABOVE: *John Pettie,* Bonnie Prince Charlie entering the Ballroom at Holyroodhouse, *1892*

'he mounted his horse and rode through St Anne's yards into Holyroodhouse amidst the cries of 60,000 people, who fill'd the air with their acclamations of joy'.

LORD ELCHO ON BONNIE PRINCE CHARLIE

THE EXILED STUARTS

JAMES VII AND II, A STAUNCH CATHOLIC, was deposed in 1689 by his Protestant daughter Mary and son-in-law William of Orange. He set up court in France and continued to maintain his claim to the throne until his death in 1701. This claim was sustained by his son, Prince James Francis Edward Stuart (1688-1766), who styled himself James VIII of Scotland and James III of England. Known also as the Old Pretender, James made a failed attempt to regain the throne in 1715. It was left to his son, Prince Charles Edward Stuart (1720–88), or Bonnie Prince Charlie as he was known, to uphold the claim.

In 1745 Charles Edward Stuart, the Young Pretender, launched an attempt to regain the crown for his father. He landed on the west coast of Scotland, raising his father's standard at Glenfinnan. With support from the Jacobite clans in the Highlands, the Prince marched through Scotland with his army and arrived in Edinburgh. He entered the Palace of Holyroodhouse, and on the same day heralds proclaimed James VIII King of Scots and his son as Regent. Four days later the Jacobites met a small British army, led by Sir John Cope, at Prestonpans, just outside the city. The result was a resounding victory for the Prince's army and he returned to Edinburgh in triumph.

The Prince was determined to march into England and left Edinburgh six weeks later. The following year, in April, the Prince and his Jacobite supporters were finally defeated by the Hanoverian army at Culloden. Bonnie Prince Charlie fled Scotland, and spent his remaining years in Europe, until his death in 1788. His brother Henry Benedict, created a cardinal in 1747, died in 1807 and the direct Stuart line finally came to an end.

CLOCKWISE FROM TOP LEFT:
Francesco Trevisani, Prince James Francis Edward Stuart, the Old Pretender, *1719–20*

Louis-Gabriel Blanchet, Prince Charles Edward Stuart, the Young Pretender, *1739*

Louis-Gabriel Blanchet, Prince Henry Benedict Stuart, Cardinal York, *c.1739*

British School, An incident at the rebellion of 1745, *c.1750*

'A long, low, and ill-proportioned gallery, hung with pictures, affirmed to be the portraits of kings, who, if they ever flourished at all, lived several hundred years before the invention of painting in oil colours, served as a sort of guard chamber or vestibule to the apartments which the adventurous Charles Edward now occupied in the palace of his ancestors'. During the evening this room became the setting for a ball and other evening entertainments, which the Prince held at the palace.

Prince Charles Edward left Edinburgh with his troops at the end of October 1745, on his way to England. Following his departure, soldiers from Edinburgh Castle arrived at the palace, and in the words of a Jacobite lady, 'They have destroy'd the apartment the Prince was in, tore down the silk bed he lay in, broke and carried off all the fine gilded glasses, cabinets and everything else.' The destruction was not complete, however. In January 1746, after defeat by the Jacobites at Falkirk, government troops billeted at the palace damaged de Wet's portraits of the Scottish kings. Before the decisive battle of Culloden, the King's son the Duke of Cumberland, commander of the troops, also stayed in the palace, occupying the same room that the Prince had recently left.

Little effort was made to maintain the palace during the 18th century and the condition of its interior gradually deteriorated. In 1758, in order to strengthen the roof of the Abbey Church, stone slabs were placed over the vaulting, but this extra weight hastened its collapse ten years later, leaving the abbey in ruins. The air of neglect which hung around the palace encouraged its development as a tourist attraction, and during the Romantic period, from the end of the 18th century, fascination grew about Mary, Queen of Scots, her apartments and the dramatic events that took place there. The servants of the Duke of Hamilton ran a profitable sideline as tour guides, escorting visitors around James V's Tower, describing in detail Rizzio's murder and the alleged bloodstain left on the floor. Many of the Duke of Hamilton's furnishings, which were deemed old-fashioned, were moved from his apartments to Mary, Queen of Scots' rooms above, including the large, late 17th-century State Bed (now in the King's Bedchamber), described by Sir Walter Scott as the 'couch of the Rose of Scotland'.

ABOVE: *Thomas Sandby, Edinburgh Panorama, 1745–6, showing Holyroodhouse from the south.*

ABOVE: Queen Mary's Bedchamber, 1862–3. *Lithograph after George M. Greig.*

"*The Old Chapel Royal, or church of the convent, stands in its dishabille, ruined and decayed, and must fall down.*"

DANIEL DEFOE, *A Tour Through the Whole Island of Great Britain, 1724-26*

ABOVE: *Sir Thomas Lawrence,* Charles X, King of France, *1825 (detail)*

THE ABBEY SANCTUARY

From the foundation of Holyrood Abbey, the precincts were a place of sanctuary, initially for all criminals, then, from the 16th century, for debtors. The sanctuary boundary at the foot of the Canongate was marked by the Girth Cross, now shown as a circle of cobbles. The enclosed area included the royal park and all inhabited houses within the abbey. Debtors, or 'abbey lairds' as they were known, were protected from the moment they crossed the sanctuary boundary, but were required to remain within on weekdays. On Sundays, when there could be no arrest, debtors could travel freely in the city, but had to return by midnight. The jurisdiction and administration of the abbey and sanctuary was carried out by the Baillie, through the Abbey Court, and the area was guarded by the constables of Holyrood, one of the oldest police forces in the world. Today the High Constables of Holyrood, as they are now known, wear a distinctive navy blue uniform and carry a baton. They form a ceremonial guard on duty when The Queen is in residence, and can be seen in the illustration on page 6.

French royalty at the palace

AT THE END OF THE 18TH CENTURY Holyroodhouse provided a home for the Comte d'Artois (1757–1836; the youngest brother of Louis XVI of France), who had been in exile since the start of the French Revolution in 1789. Artois, who had incurred large debts on the Continent, was offered refuge at the palace, where he was able to take advantage of the sanctuary it offered to debtors. He arrived in 1796 and was provided with the faded splendours of the Royal Apartments, neglected for many years – a striking contrast to his lavish former accommodation at Versailles.

Substantial refurbishment was carried out in advance of his arrival and during the following decade. Edinburgh's leading furniture makers, Young, Trotter and Hamilton, were commissioned to renovate the interior of the apartments. The work took around four months and the total bill came to just over £2,600. Tapestries were cleaned, walls were repaired and hung with canvas before being papered, carpets were laid and curtains made for windows and bed-hangings. Plain new mahogany furniture was provided, similar to that supplied to the residents of Edinburgh's elegant New Town. A private chapel was set up at one end of the Great Gallery and a billiard room was completely fitted out in the former Guard Chamber.

Artois, or 'Monsieur' as he was known, was joined at the palace by members of his family and his servants, and many of his faithful followers arrived from Europe, forming a French colony in the city of Edinburgh. Artois remained at Holyroodhouse until 1803, although the rooms continued to be occupied by members of his suite until 1815. He eventually succeeded to the French throne, as Charles X, in 1824. Following the July Revolution in 1830 and his abdication, the exiled King again took up residence at Holyroodhouse. Furniture from his apartments that had been put to use elsewhere in the palace was hastily brought out again. He finally departed two years later and remained in Europe until his death in 1836.

George IV's visit to Scotland

A TURNING POINT in the history of the palace as a royal residence came in 1822, when George IV (r.1820–30) visited Scotland. He was the first reigning monarch to visit the country since Charles I in 1633. The visit was encouraged by the Scottish writer Sir Walter Scott, who devised the King's programme and the accompanying pageantry. The neglected and dilapidated palace was not thought suitable for the King to stay in, so he was lodged seven miles away at the more comfortable Dalkeith Palace, the seat of the Duke of Buccleuch. Holyroodhouse, however, was extensively tidied up,

'In compliment to the country, his Majesty appeared in complete Highland costume, made of the Royal Stewart tartan...'.

ABOVE: *Sir David Wilkie, George IV, 1829*

GEORGE IV'S HIGHLAND DRESS

In preparation for his visit to Scotland in 1822, George IV placed an order with George Hunter & Co. of Princes Street, Edinburgh, for a complete Highland dress outfit. The kilt and plaid were made of rich red Royal Stewart tartan, and were constructed using 61 yards of satin, 31 yards of velvet and 17 yards of cashmere. The sporran was made from fine white goatskin and ornamented with the Royal Arms and Scottish thistle. The Glengarry bonnet bore a badge in the form of the Crown of Scotland set with precious stones. The usual Highland accoutrements were also supplied, including a dirk and scabbard, a broadsword, pistols and a powder horn. The total cost of the King's outfit was £1,354.

The King wore the Highland dress at his *levée* at the palace, provoking many comments. A contemporary account of the visit records, 'In compliment to the country, his Majesty appeared in complete Highland costume, made of the Royal Stewart tartan, which displayed his manly and graceful figure to great advantage'. The painter David Wilkie, who attended the reception, reported to his sister that he thought the King looked very fine in his kilt, 'with a kind of flesh-coloured pantaloons underneath'.

ABOVE: *Sir David Wilkie,* The entrance of
George IV at Holyroodhouse, *1822–29.*

To his surprise, the King experienced a rapturous welcome when he arrived at the port of Leith in August. He was received at the palace as King of Scotland in a spectacular and symbolic ceremony.

with many repairs inside and out, including the approach roads. Most of the grace-and-favour tenants were evicted for the length of the visit, and inside the palace the firm of Trotter undertook redecoration and the replacement of upholstery and furnishings. This included the fitting out of a Great Drawing Room in Charles II's old Guard Chamber. It was hung with crimson cloth fringed with gold and Queen Charlotte's throne was sent up from Buckingham House to be installed. Gas lighting illuminated the exterior of the palace and the streets of Edinburgh.

To his surprise, the King experienced a rapturous welcome when he arrived at the port of Leith in August. He was received at the palace as King of Scotland in a spectacular and symbolic ceremony. The event was recorded by the Scottish artist Sir David Wilkie. The first *levée*, or reception, was held at the palace two days later, when the King was introduced to 1,200 gentlemen, many of whom had queued for hours. Guests gathered at first in the Great Gallery and then progressed through the apartments in the reverse of the usage originally planned by Bruce, before being greeted by the King in his Drawing Room or Throne Room. George IV received his guests in full Highland dress, made especially for the visit. Later in the week the King held a Drawing Room at the palace for over 400 ladies. Other events during the visit included a Grand Procession to Edinburgh Castle, the Peer's Ball at the Assembly Rooms, the Royal Review of the Yeomanry on Portobello Beach and a service at St Giles' Cathedral. At all events the King was accompanied by his newly instituted Royal Bodyguard, the Royal Company of Archers.

Before he left Edinburgh the King paid a private visit to his palace. He was shown round Mary, Queen of Scots' apartments by the Duke of Hamilton's housekeeper, and decreed, 'in repairing the palace, these apartments should be preserved, sacred from every alteration'.

Following the King's visit, interest in the palace increased and the number of visitors swelled. Funds were found for further improvements, supervised by Sir Robert Reid, the King's Architect in Scotland. Floors were renewed and the southern end of the palace was refaced. The work included the removal of some of the more derelict outlying buildings on the north and south sides of the palace. The two-storey range built by Bruce on the north side of James V's Tower as part of the Queen's Apartments, with an interior remodelled by William Adam in the 1740s, was also demolished.

As a consequence of the improvements, in 1834 William IV decided to allow the Lord High Commissioner to the General Assembly of the Church of Scotland to take up residence for the duration of the meeting. A proposal to rebuild the Chapel Royal to house the Assembly was presented by the architect James Gillespie Graham (although actually designed by his collaborator A.W.N. Pugin), but came to nothing.

Queen Victoria and Holyroodhouse

QUEEN VICTORIA (r.1837–1901) paid her first visit to Scotland in 1842. Like her uncle George IV, she stayed at Dalkeith Palace, but was prevented from visiting Holyroodhouse by an outbreak of scarlet fever at the palace. She travelled to Perth and Stirling as well as Edinburgh. This visit engendered a deep love of the country and led to the purchase of Balmoral Castle, in Aberdeenshire, as the Queen's Highland holiday home. She described it as 'this most beautiful country which I am proud to call my own, where there was such devoted loyalty to the family

ABOVE: *This engraving of Holyroodhouse after Edward Blore, published in 1835, shows the two-storey range on the north side of the palace which was demolished after the visit of George IV.*

ABOVE: *Sir George Hayter,* Queen Victoria in Coronation Robes, *1838.*

ABOVE: *George M. Greig,* The Presence-Chamber or Evening (or Outer) Drawing Room, *1862–3*

ABOVE: *George M. Greig,* Queen Victoria's Sitting-Room or Morning Drawing Room, *1862–3. The French tapestries illustrating* The History of Diana *still hang in this room (see p.42).*

of my ancestors.' Her love of Scotland resulted in a decisive change in the fortunes of Holyroodhouse, as the palace was seen as a strategically placed stop on the long journey north to Balmoral. For the Scots, the Queen's return to the old Stuart palace was seen as an event of deep emotional significance and, gradually, Holyroodhouse was reinstated as Scotland's foremost royal residence.

The renovation of the dilapidated palace, commanded by the Queen, was supervised from London in preparation for her visit in 1850, but as the repairs were for the Queen's personal convenience, rather than for official duties, the Treasury was reluctant to grant more than a minimal sum for what they classed a 'temporary residence'. The palace was still occupied by many grace-and-favour tenants, so space was limited, and it was the old Royal Apartments on the first floor that were restored for the Queen. Robert Matheson, Principal Architect of the Office of Works in Scotland, was determined that the quality and nature of the repairs should be worthy of the palace's historical significance.

The Edinburgh firm of Trotter was engaged again, this time to strip Charles II's panelling of its later white paint. Matheson arranged for the redecoration to be carried out by David Ramsay Hay, Edinburgh's leading interior decorator, who had worked for Sir Walter Scott at Abbotsford, his home in the Scottish borders. Hay cleaned the spectacular plasterwork ceilings in the Royal Apartments and repainted them in rich colours, introducing shades that picked up the tones of the panelling and tapestries where appropriate, creating a unified effect throughout the sequence of rooms. Furniture left behind by previous tenants, together with that provided for the French visitors, was combined with pieces sent up from Buckingham Palace. These interiors were later recorded, at the Queen's request, in a series of watercolours by George M. Greig. Following Queen Victoria's first visit in 1850, improvements continued and a small sum was granted to renovate the Throne Room created for George IV. A heraldic ceiling was designed by Matheson and painted by Hay, to provide a more dignified and imposing room, but such was the shortage of space at the palace that the room had to be used by Queen Victoria as the Royal Dining Room as well. Some areas, such as the Great Gallery, remained untouched and neglected. Eventually, with the departure of most of the grace-and-favour tenants, the Queen and her family moved to apartments on the second floor, all

decorated with the 'same pretty carpets and chintzes'. Victoria paid her last visit Holyroodhouse in 1886.

ABOVE: *The new fountain in the Forecourt, installed in 1859. Lithograph after J.H. Connop.*

Improvements were also made by Matheson to the immediate surroundings of the palace, with Prince Albert taking a particular interest in these schemes. A new garden and stable buildings were created, together with a carriage approach to the north, avoiding the slum-ridden Canongate. In the Forecourt Matheson placed a fountain, modelled on the historic example at Linlithgow Palace to the west of Edinburgh.

Queen Victoria was 'struck with the beauty of the edifice', and her frequent visits to Holyroodhouse turned the tide of neglect

"We passed by Holyrood Chapel, which is old and full of interest, and Holyrood Palace, a royal-looking old place."

QUEEN VICTORIA, *Journal*, 3 September 1842

and ensured its future as a royal palace. It also brought the palace to the centre of public attention and led to a demand for visits by an inquisitive public. From 1854 the Commissioners of Works assumed responsibility for opening up parts of the palace to the general public.

The palace during the 20th century

KING EDWARD VII (r.1901–10) made a brief visit to Holyroodhouse in 1903 while staying at Dalkeith Palace. He held a *levée* in the Throne Room and made an inspection of the Royal Company of Archers. At this time the idea of restoring and re-roofing the Abbey Church was revived, with funds left for this purpose by the Earl of Leven. However, the scheme progressed no further than the design stage amidst fears that restoration might damage the historic fabric, and the abbey has remained a picturesque ruin.

OPENING THE PALACE TO VISITORS

From the mid–18th century the apartments associated with Mary, Queen of Scots were shown to visitors by successive housekeepers of the Duke of Hamilton. Following Queen Victoria's visit in 1850, the Lord Provost of Edinburgh petitioned the Queen with the request that Holyroodhouse might be opened in a similar manner to Hampton Court Palace, which had been open to the public since 1838. In 1852 arrangements were brought under the management of Robert Matheson, of the Office of Works in Scotland. Matheson entered into an agreement with the Duke of Hamilton, whereby the Duke's apartments in James V's Tower were relinquished in favour of a new suite of rooms above the Great Gallery. Staff were appointed to show what became known as the Historical Apartments on a regular basis. Tickets cost sixpence during the week, but Saturday opening was free. Visitors were taken through the Great Gallery, the recently vacated first-floor apartments, which became known as the Darnley Rooms, and Mary, Queen of Scots' apartments. Matheson also arranged for the purchase of an important collection of furniture and tapestries 'from the Royal Palaces of Scotland' from R.G. Ellis, an Edinburgh lawyer, who wished to see it preserved at Holyroodhouse.

LEFT: *Messrs Dickinson*, The first *levée* of Edward VII at the Palace of Holyroodhouse, *12 May 1903. This view shows the King in the Throne Room, a line of Scots before him, waiting to be presented. At the foot of the dais stands the Lord Chamberlain, and the Royal Company of Archers are on duty.*

It was during the reign of King George V (r.1910–36) that the palace came to life again and repairs were undertaken to ensure it became a regular royal residence and a much-loved family home. In preparation for the visit to Scotland in 1911 of the King and his consort Queen Mary, a number of changes were made, including the installation of central heating and electric light, and repairs to the drainage system, but there was so little accommodation available that temporary buildings were put up in the gardens for staff.

After the First World War a programme of improvements was implemented, overseen by J. Wilson Paterson of the Office of Works. New bathrooms were created and the kitchens were thoroughly modernised, with the provision of gas ovens and steam cookers. Electric service lifts were provided which led directly to the King and Queen's private apartments, and to the new service rooms behind the Great Gallery, allowing that room to be used as the State Dining Room when required. The State Rooms were redecorated and new panelling was installed where necessary. The Throne Room was renovated, with new thrones and canopy; a new ceiling was created and the interior was finished to harmonise with Bruce's original work throughout the palace. Queen Mary took an active part in refurnishing the rooms and the Holyrood Amenity Trust was set up in 1925 to acquire items specifically for use at the palace. At the same time the importance of Charles II's State Rooms was recognised and the public tour was extended to include these as well as Mary, Queen of Scots' apartments.

ABOVE: *Queen Mary presenting badges to Queen's Nurses in the palace gardens, with the abbey in the background, 11 July 1923.*

ABOVE: *King George VI and Queen Elizabeth, with Princess Elizabeth and Princess Margaret Rose, during an inspection of the Royal Company of Archers at Holyroodhouse, 5 July 1937.*

Her Majesty The Queen paid her first official visit to the palace shortly after her coronation in 1953.

The opportunity to enhance the external appearance of the palace was provided with the selection of Holyroodhouse as the site of the Scottish National Memorial to King Edward VII. The Forecourt was enclosed within richly decorated wrought-iron ornamental railings and gates. The statue of the King, by H.S. Gamley, faced the west front of the abbey. The memorial was unveiled by King George V in 1922.

The cost of the repairs led to a review of the palace's role and Holyroodhouse was recognised as the Sovereign's official residence in Scotland. It began to be used on a regular basis for garden parties and ceremonies such as investitures and presentations.

King George VI (r.1936–52) and his consort Queen Elizabeth were regular visitors to Scotland. The daughter of the Earl of Strathmore, Queen Elizabeth spent much of her childhood at Glamis Castle. The royal couple paid a visit to Holyroodhouse in 1937 and then continued the tradition of regular visits to the palace, usually accompanied by their daughters, Princess Elizabeth and Princess Margaret Rose. Her Majesty The Queen paid her first official visit to the palace shortly after her coronation in 1953. During the 20th century the role of the palace continued to expand and today, as the official residence of The Queen in Scotland, it is the focus of important state events as well as less formal visits by members of the Royal Family.

THE QUEEN'S GALLERY

In 2002 the new Queen's Gallery was opened to celebrate The Queen's Golden Jubilee. Benjamin Tindall Architects of Edinburgh created the Gallery in the shell of the former Holyrood Free Church and

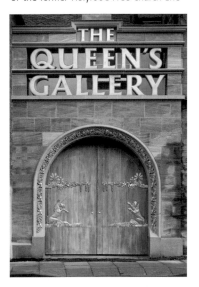

Duchess of Gordon's School at the entrance to the palace. The two buildings had been constructed in the 1840s with funds from the Duchess of Gordon, but fell into disuse later in the 19th century. The design of the gallery complements the original architecture, elements of which have been creatively incorporated into the new spaces.

The Gallery provides modern, purpose-built facilities to enable a programme of changing exhibitions of works of art from the Royal Collection to be shown in Edinburgh in tandem with exhibitions at The Queen's Gallery, Buckingham Palace.

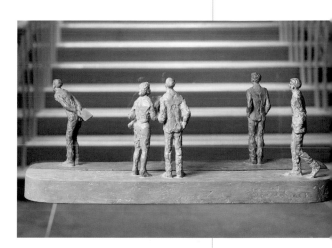

ABOVE: *One of the Gallery's patinated bronze interior door handles, by the sculptor Jill Watson. The figures look through the glass door into the Gallery.*

BELOW: *The interior of The Queen's Gallery, showing the exhibition* Canaletto in Venice *(2006–7).*

LEFT: *The entrance to The Queen's Gallery.*

CANALETTO in Venice

Tour of the Palace

Forecourt

THE VISITOR APPROACHES THE PALACE through the restored and adapted Guardhouse. Designed in a baronial style in 1861 by Robert Matheson, the Guardhouse is part of the Mews area that now includes the café and other visitor services. On entering the Forecourt the spectacular setting is immediately evident. The grounds are surrounded by 650 acres of open parkland and the view is dominated by Salisbury Crags and their highest peak, Arthur's Seat, formed from the eruption of a volcano over 350 million years ago.

The enclosed Forecourt is largely the result of progressive 19th- and 20th-century campaigns of improvement. In the centre is a large stone fountain, modelled by Matheson in 1858–9 on the 16th-century fountain at Linlithgow Palace. The wrought-iron gates and screens created by J. Starkie Gardiner and the imposing gate piers bearing the lion and unicorn were raised as part of the development of the site in 1920 for the Scottish National Memorial to Edward VII, giving a greater sense of enclosure to the Forecourt.

In July each year, at the start of The Queen's annual visit to the palace, the Forecourt is transformed into a parade ground for the Ceremony of the Keys, when the Lord Provost of Edinburgh presents The Queen with the keys to the City of Edinburgh.

ABOVE: *Detail of one the gates piers on the south side of the Forecourt.*

BELOW: *The Forecourt, fountain and entrance to the palace.*

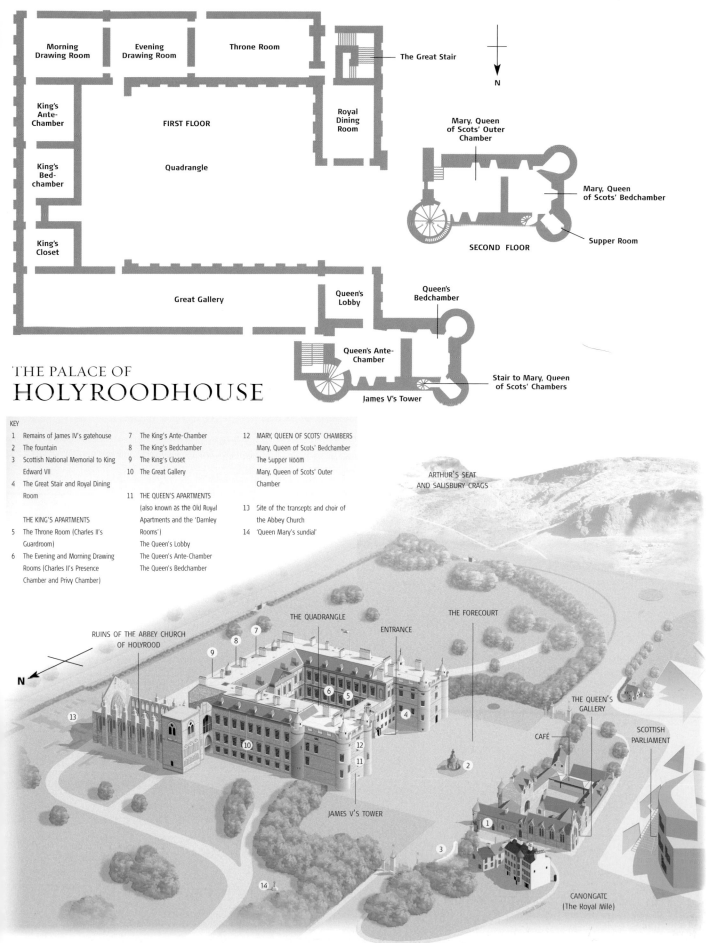

Morning
Drawing Room

Evening
Drawing Room

Throne Room

The Great Stair

N

King's
Ante-
Chamber

FIRST FLOOR

Royal
Dining
Room

King's
Bed-
chamber

Quadrangle

Mary, Queen
of Scots' Outer
Chamber

Mary, Queen
of Scots' Bedchamber

King's
Closet

Supper Room

SECOND FLOOR

Great Gallery

Queen's
Lobby

Queen's
Bedchamber

Queen's Ante-
Chamber

Stair to Mary, Queen
of Scots' Chambers

James V's Tower

THE PALACE OF
HOLYROODHOUSE

KEY

1 Remains of James IV's gatehouse
2 The fountain
3 Scottish National Memorial to King Edward VII
4 The Great Stair and Royal Dining Room

THE KING'S APARTMENTS

5 The Throne Room (Charles II's Guardroom)
6 The Evening and Morning Drawing Rooms (Charles II's Presence Chamber and Privy Chamber)

7 The King's Ante-Chamber
8 The King's Bedchamber
9 The King's Closet
10 The Great Gallery
11 THE QUEEN'S APARTMENTS (also known as the Old Royal Apartments and the 'Darnley Rooms')
The Queen's Lobby
The Queen's Ante-Chamber
The Queen's Bedchamber

12 MARY, QUEEN OF SCOTS' CHAMBERS
Mary, Queen of Scots' Bedchamber
The Supper Room
Mary, Queen of Scots' Outer Chamber

13 Site of the transepts and choir of the Abbey Church

14 'Queen Mary's sundial'

ARTHUR'S SEAT
AND SALISBURY CRAGS

RUINS OF THE ABBEY CHURCH
OF HOLYROOD

THE QUADRANGLE

THE FORECOURT

ENTRANCE

N

THE QUEEN'S
GALLERY

CAFÉ

SCOTTISH
PARLIAMENT

JAMES V'S TOWER

CANONGATE
(The Royal Mile)

The entrance front with Royal Arms of Scotland above.

Entrance Front

AT FIRST SIGHT, the façade of the palace appears to be of one date, with two massive towers at either end. Closer examination reveals the greater age of the left-hand tower, with its weathered and battered stonework. This is the oldest remaining part of the palace, built for James V in 1528–32. Decorating its walls are replica panels with the arms of James V and his Queen, Mary of Guise. It was on the second floor of this tower that their daughter, Mary, Queen of Scots, lived during the 1560s. This tower is balanced by its more regular partner on the right, erected as part of the rebuilding of the palace by Sir William Bruce for Charles II in 1671. The two-storey central block that connects the towers was built in 1676 in a classical style, and incorporates the main entrance to the palace. This was conceived as a triumphal gateway, framed by paired Doric columns and surmounted by the Royal Arms of Scotland. Above, a crowned cupola with a clock rises behind a broken pediment supported by dolphins, on which are two reclining figures.

Quadrangle

THE PALACE is laid out round this central, classical-style quadrangle, with three principal storeys on three sides and two storeys on the entrance side. The architect Sir William Bruce deployed three of the five classical orders, Doric, Ionic and Corinthian, to emphasise the

ROYAL COAT OF ARMS

Over the front entrance to the palace *(left)* is the Royal Coat of Arms of Scotland, as used before the Union of the Crowns in 1603. The shield depicts a lion rampant and the crest is a lion sitting on a crown, holding a sword and a sceptre. The supporters are two unicorns, one holding the banner of arms, the other the national flag of Scotland. Below is the motto *Nemo me impune lacessit* (No one provokes me with impunity).

On the tympanum in the Quadrangle and within the palace can be seen the Scottish version of the Royal Coat of Arms, as used in Scotland after 1603. The shield is quartered, showing the lion of Scotland in the first and fourth quarters, with those of England in the second. The unicorn supporter is given priority of place on the left.

ABOVE: *The Quadrangle.*
LEFT: *Detail of the architecture in the Quadrangle, showing the classical orders of Doric, Ionic and Corinthian.*

status of each floor, which can also be judged from the ceiling heights. The middle three bays of the eastern façade, stepped forward and crowned by a pediment enclosing the Royal Coat of Arms, indicate the location of the most important rooms in the Royal Apartments. The overall effect is one of balance, symmetry and proportion. This represented a new style of architecture in Scotland, breaking completely with the tradition of fortified houses. The grand classical design was widely admired and copied throughout the country, for example at Melville House in Fife, Hamilton Palace in Lanarkshire (now demolished) and Dalkeith Palace in Midlothian.

Great Stair

THIS IMPOSING STAIRCASE, with its stone steps and balustrade, provided the formal approach to the processional route to the Royal Apartments on the first floor and now gives visitors their first taste of the baroque interior of the palace. The cantilevered stair, at the forefront of building technology at the time, and the spectacular plasterwork ceiling, were designed to impress. The ceiling is the first in a series created by the English plasterers John Houlbert and George Dunsterfield. The decoration, built up on a timber framework, was created in moulds from plaster reinforced with horsehair, applied and finished by hand. In the corners, figures of angels bear the attributes of kingship, the Honours of Scotland: the crown, the sceptre and the sword. The central compartment, originally intended to be painted, is surrounded by tiers of hand-modelled flowers and swags creating an extraordinary three-dimensional effect. Below the ceiling are eight framed Italian fresco fragments, purchased by Prince Albert and kept at Holyroodhouse since 1881.

ABOVE: *The Great Stair.*

LEFT: *Detail of plasterwork in the ceiling above the Great Stair, showing the lifesize figure of an angel, holding the Scottish crown.*

FRESCOES BY LATTANZIO GAMBARA

The eight detached and framed fresco panels hanging above the Great Stair were painted by the North Italian artist Lattanzio Gambara (c.1530–74). Dating from c.1550, the frescoes were originally painted for the Palazzo Pedrocca in Brescia. The subjects are taken from Ovid's *Metamorphoses* and include three scenes of the *Wedding of Pirithöus and Hippodamia*. The frescoes were acquired in 1856 by Prince Albert, who wished to promote the revival of fresco painting in Britain; they provided practical examples of the technique for artists working on the decoration of the new Houses of Parliament. They were transferred on to canvas and, having served their purpose, were eventually moved to Holyroodhouse in 1881.

Lattanzio Gambara, An Allegory of Fortitude and Charity, *c.1550*

Lattanzio Gambara, Scene from the wedding of Pirithöus and Hippodamia, *c.1550*

ABOVE: The Queen receiving the Honours of Scotland, St Giles' Cathedral, Edinburgh, 24 June 1953, *by Sir Stanley Cursiter, 1954*

Pictures

Sir Stanley Cursiter, *The Queen receiving the Honours of Scotland, St Giles' Cathedral, Edinburgh, 24 June 1953*, 1954

David Donaldson, *Queen Elizabeth II*, 1967

Lattanzio Gambara, *Mercury*, c.1550

Lattanzio Gambara, *Apollo*, c.1550

Lattanzio Gambara, *Diana*, c.1550

Lattanzio Gambara, *An Allegory (Fortitude and Charity)*, c.1550

Lattanzio Gambara, *Neptune and Caenis*, c.1550

Lattanzio Gambara, *Three scenes from the wedding of Pirithöus and Hippodamia*, c.1550

Furniture

Pair of giltwood pier tables by Whytock and Reid, Edinburgh, made for two alabaster table tops formerly in the collection of Pope Pius VI. Presented to King George V in 1917

Set of carved oak side chairs, late 17th-century style

Sedan chair, late 18th century. Reputed to have belonged to the Scottish ballad writer Carolina, Baroness Nairne (1766–1845)

Arms

Two cases each containing a trophy of a pair of barbed arrows resting on a green cushion, the Reddendos presented by the Royal Company of Archers to King Edward VII in 1903, and to King George V in 1911

Two trophies of basket-hilted broadswords, 18th and 19th centuries

Tapestries

Three Flemish (Brussels) panels from the *Planets* series, late 16th century, moved from Hampton Court Palace to Holyroodhouse c.1860: *The Toilet of Venus; Bacchanalian Feast; Mars and Venus*

Flemish (Brussels) panel from *The Destruction of Troy* series, late 16th century, recorded at Holyroodhouse since 1685: *Sinon brought before Priam*

The State Apartments

Royal Dining Room

IN CHARLES II'S TIME this room was the Queen's Guard Chamber, at the start of the Queen's suite of rooms. Originally it would have been plainly finished, in keeping with this function. It was converted around 1800 into an elegant neoclassical reception room, when it formed part of the apartments of the Duke of Hamilton, the Hereditary Keeper of the Palace. Although the decorative scheme is undocumented, the high quality of the plaster mouldings and the graceful screen of Ionic columns suggest the style of the Scottish architect Robert Adam. It was first used as a dining room at the end of Queen Victoria's reign, and it is still used as such today by The Queen and other members of the Royal Family

Pictures

Sir David Wilkie, *George IV*, 1829

Jens Juel, *Frederik VI, King of Denmark*, 1784 (overdoor)

Jens Juel, *Louise Augusta, Duchess of Augustenburg*, 1784 (overdoor)

Louis-Gabriel Blanchet, *Prince Charles Edward Stuart*, 1739

Louis-Gabriel Blanchet, *Prince Henry Benedict Stuart*, *c*.1739

Sir George Hayter, *Queen Victoria in Coronation Robes*, 1838

Furniture

Mahogany five-pedestal dining table, early 19th century

Set of mahogany rail-back dining chairs, late 18th century

Pair of mid-18th-century style giltwood pier tables with marble tops

Mahogany butler's tray with brass handles by Trotter of Edinburgh, 1796

Mahogany buffet table with brass inlays, early 19th century

Porcelain

Part of a Derby dessert service, early 19th century

Pair of Coalport vases and covers decorated with Royal Coat of Arms, early 19th century

Silver

Selection of silver from an extensive banqueting service, Edinburgh, 1935

BELOW: *Laying the table in the dining room.*

JUBILEE GIFT OF SILVER

A silver banqueting service, designed for 100 guests, was presented by the Scottish benefactor Sir Alexander Grant to mark the Silver Jubilee of King George V and Queen Mary in 1935. The service, which comprises over 3,000 pieces, was commissioned specifically for use at Holyroodhouse. The design, by J. Wilson Paterson, Henry Tatton and John Cartwright, is based on Scottish examples of the early 17th century. It was made in Edinburgh by Henry Tatton of Rose Street and each piece bears the hallmark of the Edinburgh Assay Office (the three-towered castle), the commemorative Jubilee mark and the maker's mark *HT*, and is engraved with the Scottish Coat of Arms or the Scottish Royal Crest. The service includes candelabra, tureens, salvers, plates, dishes, soufflé dishes, sauceboats, ladles, knives, forks, spoons, oyster forks, asparagus tongs, teapots, milk jugs and tea trays. The gift also included damask table linen, which was decorated with the Royal Arms, the Royal Cypher and the year 1935. The silver and the table linen are still in use at the palace today.

Silver tea kettle and stand from the Jubilee gift of 1935.

Throne Room

THIS WAS THE KING'S GUARD CHAMBER in Charles II's palace, the first room of the elegant processional route which eventually led to the King's Bedchamber. The route was designed to ensure that access to the royal presence could be strictly controlled. The Throne Room was plainly finished originally, with a simple cornice. It has been much altered subsequently, and its use has changed more than any other room in the palace.

In 1822, for George IV's visit to Scotland, it became the King's Great Drawing Room, where he held *levées*, or receptions. It was hung with crimson cloth and the throne and canopy made for Queen Charlotte, the King's mother, was transported from Buckingham House. The placing of the throne canopy at the western end of the room entailed the reversal of the processional route created by Sir William Bruce for Charles II.

A new plaster ceiling bearing the Royal Arms was installed here for Queen Victoria in 1856, to give the room greater dignity.

ABOVE: *The Throne Room.*

BELOW: *Pair of upholstered throne chairs made for King George V and Queen Mary in 1911.*

ORDER OF THE THISTLE

The Most Ancient and Most Noble Order of the Thistle is the highest order of chivalry in Scotland. It was James VII and II who firmly established the Order in 1687, to reward Scottish peers who supported the king. The number of Knights was limited to twelve. Queen Anne revived the Order in 1703 and the early Hanoverian kings made use of it to reward Scottish nobility. Attention was drawn to the Order when George IV wore the insignia of the Thistle during his visit to Scotland in 1822; following this, a statute established the complement of Knights at sixteen.

The Queen is Sovereign of the Order and personally appoints Knights Brethren of the Thistle. The Order honours distinguished Scottish men and (from 1987) women who have contributed in a particular way to national life. The number of Knights remains at sixteen, together with three Royal Knights. Appointments are announced on St Andrew's Day (30 November) and the installation of a new Knight takes place at a service in St Giles' Cathedral, Edinburgh, in July.

In 1687 James VII commanded that the Abbey Church be converted into the Chapel of the Order and new stalls and furnishings were designed for this purpose. The abbey and its contents were pillaged by a mob of rioters in 1688 and it was not until 1911 that the Order had its own chapel, at St Giles' Cathedral, designed by Robert Lorimer.

The insignia of the Order consists of a collar, badge and star. The motto is *Nemo me impune lacessit*. The patron saint of the Order is St Andrew, who appears on the badge.

RIGHT: *Double-sided diamond mounted Thistle Badge.*

BELOW: *Diamond-set Thistle Star, c.1820.*

Until Queen Victoria managed to remove the grace-and-favour tenants from their apartments, this room was also used as her dining room.

Queen Mary described this ceiling as 'dreadful' and the room was altered again in 1929, to the designs of J. Wilson Paterson of the Office of Works. A new ceiling was installed to reflect the character of the Charles II originals, and oak panelling, incorporating paintings, was applied to the walls. A recess was created at the west end of the room for the new thrones.

Today the Throne Room is used for receptions and other state occasions. In this room The Queen holds a luncheon for the Knights and Ladies of the Order of the Thistle, on the occasion of the installation of a new Knight.

Pictures

Daniel Mytens, *Charles I*, 1628

Sir Peter Lely, *Charles II*, c.1670

Sir Peter Lely, *Catherine of Braganza*, c.1663–5

Paul van Somer, *James VI & I*, 1618

Sir Peter Lely, *Mary of Modena when Duchess of York*, c.1675–80

Sir Peter Lely, *James VII & II when Duke of York*, c.1665

Furniture

Set of giltwood X-frame stools, 19th century (copying a set made in 1715 by Henry Williams for Hampton Court Palace)

Pair of ebonised pier tables with gilt-bronze mounts and marble tops, early 19th century

Pair of satinwood fluted pedestals, mid-19th century

Pair of upholstered throne chairs made for King George V and Queen Mary by Morris & Co. of London, 1911

Part of a set of oak window stools with needlework covers made to celebrate the Coronation of King George VI and Queen Elizabeth, 1937

Pair of gilt metal chandeliers, copied from early 18th-century silver originals by Francis Garthorne at Hampton Court Palace

Evening Drawing Room

THIS ROOM WAS THE PRESENCE CHAMBER of Charles II's palace, where important visitors would have been received by the King. This use is reflected in the impressive plasterwork ceiling by Houlbert and Dunsterfield, with its whirling scrolls set against panels of interwoven laurel branches, within a quatrefoil border of oak leaves. As with many of the other ceilings in the palace, the central decorative painting was never executed. The red marble chimneypiece is one of a number in the palace to use exotic marbles of various colours. The chimney pieces were purchased in London by an agent of the Duke of Lauderdale and add to the feeling of opulence throughout.

Queen Victoria arranged for the four tapestries to be sent up from Buckingham Palace in 1851 to give the room an air of richness and warmth. During her residence the room was used by the court as a drawing room.

Under the direction of King George V and Queen Mary, the room was redecorated and oak panelling replaced the wallpaper, which had been put up in the 18th century. The Victorian plate-glass windows were replaced with their original small panes and astragals.

Today The Queen and other members of the Royal Family use this room for receptions.

TOP: *The Evening Drawing Room.*

ABOVE. *Detail of Beauvais tapestry, c.1745, on the back of a French giltwood armchair.*

Pictures

Sir William Hutchinson, *Queen Elizabeth The Queen Mother*, 1967

Furniture

Set of six French giltwood armchairs and settee by Etienne Saint-Georges, upholstered in Beauvais tapestry woven with scenes from the *Fables* of Jean de la Fontaine, *c.*1745

Mahogany snap-top tripod table, late 18th century

Pair of gilt gesso side tables, early 18th century

Giltwood side table of 18th-century design

Part of a set of oak window stools with needlework covers made to celebrate the Coronation of King George VI and Queen Elizabeth, 1937

Silver-plated chandelier, copied from an 18th-century silver original by Francis Garthorne at Hampton Court Palace

Tapestries

Two Flemish (Brussels) panels from *The Four Continents* series, workshop of Peter and Franz van der Borght, *c.*1750, formerly at Buckingham Palace, sent to Holyroodhouse in 1851: *Asia, Africa*

Two Flemish (Brussels) 'Teniers' panels, workshop of Franz van der Borght, *c.*1750, formerly at Buckingham Palace, sent to Holyroodhouse in 1851: *The Vegetable Market; The Fish Market*

TOP: *Flemish (Brussels) tapestry of 'Africa',* c.*1750 (detail)*

ABOVE: *Flemish (Brussels) tapestry of 'Asia',* c.*1750 (detail)*

TAPESTRY COLLECTION

In the 16th and 17th centuries, tapestries were the main decorative component of royal residences, but they were only displayed when the monarch was in residence. Although 13 sets of tapestries were recorded at Holyroodhouse when Mary, Queen of Scots arrived in 1561, none of these survive at the palace. Most were still hanging when James VI was resident, but after his departure for London in 1603 many went missing and the condition of some deteriorated beyond repair. In 1633, tapestries were borrowed to hang in the palace and the abbey for Charles I's coronation. The Duke of York, the future James VII and II, brought his own furnishings, including tapestries, when he was resident in the palace between 1679 and 1682.

An inventory compiled in 1685, following the death of Charles II, recorded two sets of tapestries which are still hanging at the palace: the *History of Diana* and the *Destruction of Troy*. Tapestries were also noted as hanging in the apartments of the grace-and-favour residents by 1700, including the two Brussels panels of *Alexander the Great* and the four panels of the *Story of Tobit* in the Marquess of Breadalbane's apartment. These were purchased from the Marquess in 1860, when he finally relinquished his apartments at Holyroodhouse, and they are still in the palace today.

Many tapestries were brought to Holyroodhouse in the 19th century. Queen Victoria took a lively interest in furnishing the palace, as she and her growing family stayed there regularly on their way to and from Balmoral. In 1851 the 18th-century tapestries of *Africa* and *Asia* were brought up from Buckingham Palace and four late 16th-century panels of *The Planets* were dispatched from Hampton Court. A number of others, previously on loan to the South Kensington (later Victoria and Albert) Museum, were sent to Holyroodhouse in 1882, on the instruction of Queen Victoria. These included the Mortlake *Diogenes* panels, which had originally been purchased for Charles II in 1683.

The tapestry collection is an integral part of the history of the palace and there is now an active programme of care and conservation of this historic collection.

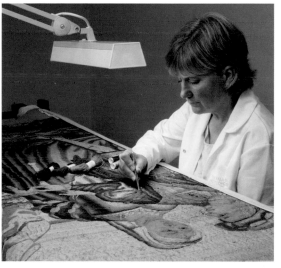

ABOVE: *Tapestry conservation work in progress.*

LEFT: *French (Paris) tapestry of 'The Birth of Diana', c.1630 (detail).*

ABOVE: *The Morning Drawing Room*

LEFT: *Detail of the plasterwork ceiling, showing the cypher of Charles II.*

Detail of a heraldic unicorn on the plasterwork ceiling.

Morning Drawing Room

THIS SUMPTUOUSLY DECORATED ROOM was originally Charles II's Privy Chamber. The rich interior indicates the exclusive use of the room, where only privileged visitors would have been allowed more private access to the King.

The ornate ceiling is richly decorated in the corners with cherubs and eagles bearing the cypher of Charles II and the Honours of Scotland. The long central panels feature heraldic lions and unicorns springing from delicately modelled rosebuds, while the swags which enclose the central compartment appear to be held to the ceiling by ribbons. The 17th-century panelling incorporates in the overmantel elaborate foliate carvings by the Dutchman, Jan van Santvoort, which enclose a painting by his compatriot, Jacob de Wet, the first in a series of overmantel paintings in the palace by this artist. Corinthian pilasters frame the dark green marble chimneypiece.

The walls are hung with French tapestries illustrating the story of the hunting goddess, Diana, purchased for Charles II in 1668. They have been hanging here since at least 1796, when this was one of several rooms used by the Comte d'Artois, the future Charles X of France.

The room was extensively renovated in 1850 for Queen Victoria, when the Edinburgh decorator D.R. Hay painted the ceiling in rich colours to complement the tapestries. Queen Victoria used the room as her private drawing room; at the time, Jacob de Wet's painting was thought unsuitable and was covered with mirror glass. During the renovations carried out for King George V and Queen Mary, the colourful ceiling was painted out in white.

Today The Queen uses the room to give private audiences, for example to receive the First Minister of Scotland, the Lord High Commissioner and other visiting dignitaries. It was in this room in 1999 that The Queen appointed the late Donald Dewar as the inaugural First Minister of the newly devolved Scottish Parliament.

ABOVE: *Detail of embroidery on the back of the chair illustrated below.*

BELOW: *Chair covered with silk and wool embroidery, mid-18th century.*

ABOVE: *Mahogany settee covered with silk and wool embroidery, upholstered by John Schaw of Edinburgh, c.1710.*

ABOVE: *The Queen presents Donald Dewar with the Royal Warrant of Appointment which confirmed him as First Minister in the Scottish Parliament, 1999.*

Pictures

Jacob de Wet, *Morning at the bath*, c.1675

Furniture

Set of mahogany side chairs with embroidered covers, mid-18th century. Formerly in the possession of Lord Adam Gordon, inherited from his mother, Henrietta, Duchess of Gordon, and in his apartments at Holyroodhouse until his death in 1801. The set was extended and new covers embroidered by the Ladies of Scotland for Queen Mary in the 1920s. The embroiderer's name is inscribed on a brass plate attached to the back of each chair

Mahogany tripod polescreen with contemporary needlework, mid-18th century

Mahogany settee with cover embroidered in silk and wool, c.1740. Upholstered by John Schaw of Edinburgh, whose initials are painted on the canvas backing

Pair of giltwood pier tables and glasses, the tables with arms and heraldic supporters of the Duchess of Gordon, mother of Lord Adam Gordon, c.1770. Recorded at Holyroodhouse since 1782

Silver-plated chandelier, copied from an 18th-century silver original by Francis Garthorne at Hampton Court Palace

Tapestries

Three French (Paris) panels from *The History of Diana* series, c.1630, recorded at Holyroodhouse in 1685:
Niobe protests at the worship of Latona; Diana between the Giants and Actaeon turned into a stag; Diana petitions Jupiter

Flemish (probably Oudenaarde) panel from *The Story of Tobit* series, early 17th century: *Tobit and Anna*

King's Ante-Chamber

THE DECORATION OF THIS ROOM is more restrained, to suit its smaller scale and function. It originally served as a waiting room to the King's Bedchamber beyond and has impressive views over the garden. The ceiling is ornamented with grotesque, clawed monsters in the corners and deep borders of fruit and foliage. Above the pink and white marble chimneypiece is one of a series of overmantel paintings by Jacob de Wet, *The Triumph of Galatea*.

In 1850 this room was Queen Victoria's bedroom, but a more convenient suite of rooms was arranged for her on the floor above once it had been vacated by its grace-and-favour tenant, the Duke of Argyll, in 1871.

Pictures

Jacob de Wet, *The Triumph of Galatea*, *c*.1675

Furniture

Ten ebonised side chairs upholstered in modern red velvet, late 17th century. Formerly in the Paulet collection, Hinton House, Somerset

Oyster-veneered walnut cabinet on stand, late 17th century

Cut-glass eight-branch chandelier, mid-18th century

Writing table, 18th century

Porcelain

Two pairs of Chinese export porcelain hexagonal vases, 18th century

Tapestries

Flemish (Brussels) panel from *The Destruction of Troy*, late 16th century, recorded at Holyroodhouse since 1685:
The death of Dido

French (Gobelins) panel from *Daphnis and Chloë* series, designed by Etienne Jeaurat, *c*.1745, sent to Holyroodhouse in 1882:
The marriage feast of Daphnis and Chloë

French (Paris) panel from *The History of Diana*, *c*.1630 (*en suite* with three in the Morning Drawing Room), recorded at Holyroodhouse since 1685:
The destruction of the children of Niobe

ABOVE: Enfilade *from the Morning Drawing Room to the Great Gallery on the east side of the palace.*

King's Bedchamber

DESIGNED AS CHARLES II'S BEDCHAMBER, this room is the culmination of the processional route through the palace. Its great importance is emphasised by the room's position on the central axis of the building, like Louis XIV's bedchamber at the French royal palace of Versailles. The lavish decoration reinforces its significance: the room contains the finest plasterwork, decorative painting and carving in the palace. It was intended to be seen by only the most privileged visitors.

The ceiling is the only one in the palace to have been completed with a central decorative panel, painted by Jacob de Wet in 1673 with *Hercules admitted to Olympus*. The realistic sky is peopled with gods raising Hercules to join them. The animals peering down over the parapet into the room add to the illusion and include owls, sheep and dogs. This central panel is enclosed by elaborate decorative plasterwork, which includes the crowned Thistle of Scotland. The overmantel painting, also by de Wet, continues the flattering comparison of Charles II with Hercules, where the infant hero is seen strangling one of the serpents sent to kill

ABOVE: *Ceiling painting in the King's Bedchamber, Hercules admitted to Olympus, by Jacob de Wet, c.1675.*

him. The rich carved surround of the overmantel and the lions framing the marble chimneypiece are as elaborate as the ceiling decoration.

From 1850 until his death in 1861 this was Prince Albert's dressing room. A contemporary watercolour shows his portable shower installed in the corner of the room.

The principal focus of the room is now the State Bed, recorded in the Duke of Hamilton's apartments at Holyroodhouse from 1684. In 1976 the bed was restored and rehung with red damask to match the original fabric.

TOP: *The King's Bedchamber.*

LEFT: *Detail of ceiling painting.*

STATE BED

This bed was not originally the King's bed, but was made for the Duke of Hamilton, the Hereditary Keeper of the Palace, and was part of the furnishings of his grace-and-favour apartment from 1684 until 1740, when a new bed was ordered. The bed was moved to Mary, Queen of Scots' Bedchamber, on the second floor of James V's Tower, where, in its tattered state, it was described as Queen Mary's bed. Many 19th-century depictions of this room show the bed in place (see illustration on p.19).

The bed underwent extensive conservation in 1976. The original red damask survives on the headboard, the cornice and the canopy. The curtains and bedcover, which had disintegrated in the 19th century, were replaced.

RIGHT: *Detail of the canopy*

Pictures

Jacob de Wet, *The infant Hercules strangling the serpents*, c.1675

Jacob de Wet, *Hercules admitted to Olympus*, c.1675

Furniture

State Bed with crimson damask upholstery (largely renewed), c.1680

Three lacquered and ebonised armchairs and one side chair, with modern upholstery, late 17th century

Walnut pier table, inlaid with panels of floral marquetry, late 17th century

Walnut pier table, late 17th century

Two pairs of walnut candlestands, late 17th century

Walnut pier glass, inlaid with panels of floral marquetry, 17th century

Walnut pier glass with pierced cresting, late 17th century

Walnut long-case clock by J. Windmills, London, early 18th century

Porcelain

Two Chinese blue and white bowls, 18th century

Tapestries

Two Flemish (Brussels) panels from *The History of Alexander* series, workshop of Jan Leyniers, mid-17th century, recorded at Holyroodhouse since 1700:
Alexander wounded in the thigh
The lion hunt

French panel, probably Gobelins, 18th century:
Figures in a landscape

Pair of French panels, probably Beauvais, c.1700, intended to be hung between windows (*entre fenêtres*)

LEFT: *Detail of the carved lion's head on the fireplace surround.*

RIGHT: *George M. Greig,* The Prince Consort's sitting room and dressing room, *1863. Prince Albert's shower-bath is on the left and his slippers can be seen by the chaise-longue.*

Lobby

THIS SMALL DOMED LOBBY led to the King's Stool Room, which contained only his close-stool, or water closet, but the decoration is still richly executed. The room had its own service stair. In 1850 it was occupied by Prince Albert's valet.

King's Closet

DESIGNED AS THE KING'S STUDY, the private character of this room is reflected in its small size. The coved ceiling incorporates the Royal Coat of Arms, paired with fantastic cartouches of Charles II's cypher, and the spandrels are decorated with military trophies, a theme echoed in the carvings of antique armour framing the overmantel. Jacob de Wet's painting depicts *The Finding of Moses*, which, by alluding to the mythical descent of the Scottish kings from Pharaoh's daughter Scota, emphasises the legendary antiquity of the royal house of Scotland. The panelled walls are hung closely with tapestries, in the 17th-century manner.

ABOVE: *Detail of the overmantel carving in the King's Closet.*

BELOW: *A corner of the King's Closet.*

RIGHT: *The Great Gallery, the largest room in the palace is often used for investitures, dinners and receptions.*

In 1850 this room became Queen Victoria's Breakfast Room, and at the time was hung with green and gold flock wallpaper.

Pictures

Jacob de Wet, *The finding of Moses*, c.1675

Furniture

Two lacquered and ebonised armchairs, a winged chair and two side chairs, with modern upholstery, late 17th century

Lacquered two-manual harpsichord with false inscription of Johannes Ruckers of Antwerp and date of 1636. French, mid-18th century

Black lacquered and gilt harp by Holzman, Paris, early 19th century

Chinese lacquer cabinet, 18th century, on later ebonised stand

Ebonised and silvered pier table with mermaid and dolphin legs, late 17th century

Pair of carved and giltwood candlestands, late 17th century

Chinese export lacquer screen, 18th century

Carved limewood pier glass, late 17th century

Tapestries

Five English (Mortlake) panels of *The life of Diogenes*, late 17th century, purchased for Charles II in 1683: *Diogenes visited by Plato;* *Diogenes meditating;* *Diogenes writing on the wall;* *The meeting of Diogenes and Alexander;* *Diogenes beside his barrel*

Great Gallery

THE LARGEST ROOM IN THE PALACE, the Great Gallery connects the King's Apartments on the east side with the Queen's Apartments in James V's Tower to the west. The view from the east windows, revealing a mass of buttresses, draws attention to the close proximity of the abbey. Sir William Bruce devised a simple classical scheme for the room, which features a pair of black marble chimneypieces within Doric surrounds, framed by Ionic pilasters. The most notable decorative feature of the room is the extensive series of portraits, hung on every wall, of real and legendary kings of Scotland, supplied by Jacob de Wet between 1684 and 1686.

The Great Gallery has served many purposes over the years. After the Union of Parliaments in 1707 it was used for the election of delegates from among Scotland's peers to attend Parliament in Westminster. In 1745, during the Jacobite occupation of Edinburgh, Prince Charles Edward Stuart held a ball in this room. A few months later, government forces were quartered here. While the Comte d'Artois, the future Charles X, was in residence, a Catholic chapel was established in the Great Gallery.

KINGS OF SCOTLAND

In 1684 the Dutch painter Jacob de Wet (c.1640–97) signed a contract to paint the portraits of 110 kings of Scotland. It is probable that the Duke of York, the future James VII and II, who was then resident at the palace, was behind the commission. Illustrating both real and legendary kings, from Fergus I in 330 BC to Charles II, the series was essentially a political statement to promote the long line of the Stuart dynasty in the newly built royal palace.

Jacob de Wet, who came to Scotland in 1673, was initially employed by the architect Sir William Bruce to paint a series of overmantels in the palace. The final contract for the kings of Scotland commission was signed in 1684, when de Wet agreed to spend two years on the paintings for a payment of £120 per year. Due to the death of Charles II before the completion of the job, de Wet was asked to paint an additional portrait of the new king, James VII, for the sum of £30.

ABOVE: *Jacob de Wet, Fergus I, 1684-6.*

The precedent for a series of paintings of the kings of Scotland had been set by the artist George Jamieson (c.1587–1644) when he produced a series of portraits of Scottish kings for Charles I's coronation in Edinburgh in 1633.

The only Stuart to use the Gallery for its intended purpose was Prince Charles Edward in 1745, when he held a ball surrounded by the portraits of his ancestors. But following the Jacobites' victory at the battle of Falkirk in January 1746, government troops under General Hawley were billeted at the palace and damaged the portraits of the Scottish kings. An anonymous journal records that the troops 'exercised the fury of their swords upon the fine pictures of many of the kings of Scotland for the defeat they received at Falkirk from their lineal descendants'. Especial violence was reserved for the portrait of Mary, Queen of Scots, the only queen in the series.

The portraits were repaired and by 1826, 'after having been moved from their hanging frames, fixed in the panels of the wainscoting', although a number still hung loose in the window embrasures at the end of the 19th century.

A programme of cleaning and restoration was completed in 2003.

Early in the 20th century, King George V improved the service arrangements between the ground floor, where the kitchens are located, and the first floor, in order for the Gallery to be used as the State Dining Room. In 1968, when the floors of the rooms above were strengthened, the opportunity was taken to install a new ceiling to improve on the room's tunnel-like appearance.

Today the Great Gallery is used regularly by The Queen to carry out investitures for Scottish recipients of honours. It is also used for state banquets, dinners and receptions.

Pictures

Jacob de Wet, 96 individual portraits of the kings of Scotland, from Fergus I to James VII, 1684–6, from the original series of 111 portraits

Furniture

Group of oak, walnut and beech cane-seated chairs, late 17th century

'TAM O'SHANTER' CHAIR

This oak chair is closely associated with the great Scottish poet Robert Burns. The back of the chair is decorated with brass plaques on which are engraved the lines of Burns' poem, *Tam O'Shanter*. The chair is made from the timbers of the Kirk at Alloway, Burns' birthplace; when the roof of the church collapsed at the end of the 18th century its timbers were reused to make items associated with Burns. The chair was acquired by George IV in 1822, the year of his visit to Scotland. It was sent to Holyroodhouse by King Edward VII in 1901.

Queen's Lobby

THIS IS THE FIRST OF THE ROOMS which formed the old Royal Apartments in James V's Tower, and which were refitted in 1671 to serve as the Queen's Apartments, designed for Catherine of Braganza, Charles II's Queen, but never inhabited by her. This room was intended as the Queen's Privy Chamber, although the name was rarely used. Sir William Bruce imposed order on the old, irregular room and a newly installed marble chimneypiece was framed by a pair of Ionic pilasters. The character of this and the following rooms remains simple, however, especially in contrast with the baroque splendour of the King's Apartments. The 17th-century plaster ceiling, with its minimal mouldings of a central star and *CR* monograms in the corners, was installed by Scottish craftsman James Baine.

In 1684 the Queen's Apartments were appropriated by the Duke of Hamilton, as Hereditary Keeper of the Palace, and this room became the Duke's Ante-Chamber.

Furniture

'Tam O'Shanter' chair, carved oak with brass panels, early 19th century (see left)

Bog oak chair, 1850, made by Curran and Sons of Lisburn, Co. Antrim, exhibited at the Great Exhibition of 1851 (see right)

Tapestries

Two Flemish (Antwerp) panels from *The Story of Semiramis* series, late 17th century: *Semiramis levelling the roads*; *Triumph of Semiramis*

RIGHT: *Bog oak chair, 1850.*

Pictures

Adriaen Hanneman, *William Hamilton, Earl of Lanark and 2nd Duke of Hamilton*, 1650

Sir Peter Lely, *Princess Isabella*, c.1677 (overdoor)

Jean-Baptiste Monnoyer, *Still life with monkey, flowers and fruit*, late 17th century (overdoor)

Jean-Baptiste Monnoyer, *Still life with squirrel, flowers and fruit in a landscape*, late 17th century (overdoor)

Queen's Ante-Chamber

TOP: *The Queen's Ante-Chamber.*

ABOVE: *English (Mortlake) tapestry from the 'The Playing Boys' series, seventeenth century (detail).*

THIS ROOM AND THE ONE FOLLOWING (the Queen's Bedchamber) were originally part of the King's Apartments in James V's Tower and, during the 1560s, were lived in by Lord Darnley, second husband of Mary, Queen of Scots. Following the rebuilding of the palace by Sir William Bruce, they became part of the Queen's Apartments, but the only royal occupant was Mary of Modena, when Duchess of York, during the period 1679–82. This room was remodelled by Bruce after 1671, with the black marble chimneypiece framed by a pair of Ionic pilasters, but the great thickness of the walls is still evident, revealing the ancient defensive origins of this part of the palace.

The Duke of Hamilton took over the rooms in James V's Tower from 1684, and by the early 18th century this room was the Duke's Dining Room, furnished with elegant Georgian furniture. Later in the century any outmoded furniture, particularly that from the Baroque period, was moved upstairs to the apartments on the second floor of the tower, formerly occupied by Mary, Queen of Scots. There they were included in the guided tours conducted by the Duke of Hamilton's servants. In due course the Duke also allowed visitors to view the first-floor rooms as part of their tour, and these became known as the Darnley Rooms.

TURKEY WORK CHAIRS

These chairs, made in the second half of the 17th century, are upholstered with Turkey work, a type of seat covering with a knotted woollen pile and colourful designs of stylised flowers on a dark background, in imitation of Turkish carpets. The chairs are survivors of extensive consignments purchased to furnish the meeting room of the Privy Council of Scotland at Holyroodhouse. The first group was acquired in 1668 by the Earl (later Duke) of Lauderdale and shipped from London. In 1685, in the newly built palace, the Council Chamber was refurnished and a further quantity of chairs was purchased for 15 shillings each, for use by members of the Privy Council. They were supplied with loose covers of green baize. Following the Act of Union in 1707, which united the Scottish and English parliaments, the Privy Council was abolished. The chairs continued to be used and were carried to St Giles' Cathedral or the Session House and back to Holyroodhouse for certain ceremonies.

When responsibility for showing the Historical Apartments passed to the Commissioners of Works in 1854, the rooms were redecorated and the panelling was grained 'in imitation of old oak'. New furniture and tapestries were acquired for the room from the collection assembled by the Edinburgh lawyer, R.G. Ellis. The tapestries and some of this furniture remain on display in this room.

Pictures (left to right)

Francesco Fieravino, *Still Life of fruit and flowers with a carpet*, c.1640–60 (overdoor)

British School, *An incident in the rebellion of 1745*, c.1750 (overdoor)

Francesco Trevisani, *Prince James Francis Edward Stuart*, c.1719–20

Italian School, *James 'the Admirable' Crichton*, 1560–85

After Cornelius van Poelenburgh, *Seven children of the King and Queen of Bohemia*, c.1630

French School, *Marie de Medici*, 17th century

Follower of Jan Weenix, *A partridge and a pigeon with instruments of the chase*, c.1718

Attributed to Frans Pourbus the Younger, *Henry IV of France*, c.1580–1610

Follower of Jan Weenix, *A woodpigeon, a partridge and a green finch with instruments of the chase*, c.1718

Anonymous, *Anne of Austria*, 17th century

Bartholomeus van Bassen, *The King and Queen of Bohemia dining in public*, c.1634

Furniture

Flemish oak-veneered cabinet, with marquetry decoration, early 17th century

Part of a group of walnut or beech side chairs with original Turkey-work upholstery, late 17th century

Dutch marquetry table, 17th century

German marquetry cabinet, late 16th century, on later English walnut stand

Dutch marquetry table, 19th century

Tapestries

Four English (Mortlake) panels of *The Playing Boys* series, first half of the 17th century

Queen's Bedchamber

ORIGINALLY this room was the King's Bedroom. When it became part of the Queen's Apartments in the 1670s it was probably the Queen's Dressing Room and was remodelled by Bruce, with a chimneypiece framed by Corinthian pilasters. The bedchamber lay to the north, in a new range of accommodation added by 1679, which also provided service rooms.

The interior was remodelled for the Duke of Hamilton by the Scottish architect William Adam, together with the bedchamber in the adjacent range, which was taken over by the Duchess of Hamilton. This range was eventually demolished in the 1820s.

The bed on display in this room, originally supplied to the Duke of Hamilton in 1682, was moved here from the second floor in the early 20th century.

THE 'DARNLEY' BED

This richly decorated tester bed, with its canopy covered with crimson and gold velvet and festoons of silk fringe, surmounted by four velvet-covered vases topped with ostrich feathers, was supplied to the Duke of Hamilton, the Hereditary Keeper of the Palace, in 1682, by the London upholsterer John Ridge for £218.10.0.

In 1745, Prince Charles Edward Stuart (Bonnie Prince Charlie) occupied the Duke of Hamilton's apartments and slept in this bed. Shortly afterwards it was used by his adversary the Duke of Cumberland.

During the later 18th century, when the Hamiltons acquired more fashionable furniture, this bed was moved to Mary, Queen of Scots' Outer Chamber, where it was described by guides as Charles I's bed. The red damask State Bed, now on display in the King's Bedchamber, was in the adjacent room and described as Mary, Queen of Scots' bed. During the 1860s, when Lord Darnley's apartments on the floor below were renovated, the bed was moved down and it became known as Lord Darnley's Bed.

The bed has undergone conservation and is placed behind glass with reduced light levels to protect the fragile textiles. The bedcover, applied with chinoiserie embroidery in silk and metal thread, was probably made in England around 1700. At the time it was presented to Edward VII in 1910 it was thought to have belonged to Henry VIII and Anne Boleyn.

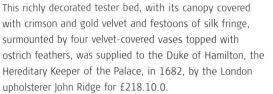

Detail of embroidered bedcover, c.1700.

Pictures
(left to right)

Anonymous, *Prince Henry Benedict Stuart (Cardinal York)*, second half of the 18th century (overdoor)

Alexis-Simon Belle, *Prince James Francis Edward Stuart with his sister, Princess Louisa Maria Theresa*, 1699 (overdoor)

British School, *Mary, Queen of Scots*, 1603–35

William Wissing, *James Duke of Cambridge*, c.1685

Copy after Sir Peter Paul Rubens, *Meleager and Atlanta* c.1640

Copy after Sir Peter Paul Rubens, *Christ in the house of Simon*, c.1640

Flemish School (after Taddeo Zuccaro), *Adoration of the Shepherds*, c.1600

Furniture and textiles

Tester bed upholstered in crimson and gold velvet and yellow satin (part renewed), c.1682

Bedcover, embroidered in silk and metal thread, c.1700

Two ebonised wing chairs, modern upholstery, late 17th century

Tapestries

French (Beauvais) panel, *Marriage of Anne of Brittany and Charles VIII of France*, second half of the 17th century

Turret Room
(left to right)

Italian School, *Portrait of a young man*, 1625–35

After Alexis-Simon Belle, *Prince James Francis Edward Stuart*, 18th century

Painted plaster bust of

Charles I, the face after Gianlorenzo Bernini, late 17th century

British School, *A memorial painting of Charles I*, 17th century

French School, *Prince James Francis Edward Stuart*, 1695–1705

Mary, Queen of Scots' Chambers

THESE ROOMS on the second floor of James V's Tower were occupied by James V's daughter, Mary, Queen of Scots, from 1561 until 1567. It was here, in the Queen's private apartments, that the brutal murder of Mary's secretary, the Italian David Rizzio, took place on 9 March 1566. The association of these rooms at Holyroodhouse with Mary's turbulent reign and this dramatic event has fascinated and thrilled visitors since the eighteenth century.

Mary, Queen of Scots' Bedchamber and Supper Room

THE SMALL SPIRAL STAIRCASE leads up to Mary, Queen of Scots' Bedchamber, so the rooms are viewed in the reverse of their intended formal sequence. The Queen's tiny supper room can be seen in the turret just off the Bedchamber. It was here that the Queen, her ladies and her secretary David Rizzio were dining on the night that Rizzio was murdered.

ABOVE: *François Clouet, Mary, Queen of Scots, c.1558–60.*

BELOW: *Mary, Queen of Scots' Bedchamber.*

BELOW LEFT: *Detail of the fine panelled ceiling.*

The bedchamber has a compartmented oak ceiling, probably dating from the mid-16th century. The initials *IR* and *MR* on the panels are those of James V and his Queen, Mary of Guise, the parents of Mary, Queen of Scots. Below the ceiling is a deep frieze, painted in grisaille with the Honours of Scotland, arabesques and cornucopia. It was painted in 1617, in imitation of the fashion for decorative plasterwork, in honour of James VI's return visit to Scotland.

When the palace was remodelled by Bruce in the 1670s, the Queen's Apartments were relocated to the floor below and the second-floor rooms fell into disuse. They were later appropriated by the Duke of Hamilton, the Hereditary Keeper of the Palace.

Mary, Queen of Scots' Bedchamber

Pictures
(from left to right)

School of Lucas
Cranach the Elder, *The
Adoration of the Magi*,
c.1540

Andrea Schiavone, *The
Adoration of the Kings*,
c.1560

After Lucas van
Leyden, *St Jerome in
his study*, c.1650

Style of Francesco
Albani, *A woman
listening to a satyr
piping*, c.1650

Flemish School, *A
dying saint*, 17th
century

Willem Key, *Lazzaro
Spinola*, 1566

Flemish School, *The
Head of Christ*, 17th
century

Flemish School, *The
Head of the Virgin*,
17th century

British School, *James VI
and I*, 17th century

Samuel Swarbreck,
*Mary Queen of Scots'
bedroom,
Holyroodhouse*, 1861

After Titian, *The Penitent
Magdalen*, c.1600

French School,
*Archibald Douglas,
6th Earl of Angus*,
16th century

British School, *Richard II*,
17th century

After Polidoro da
Caravaggio, *Putti with
goats*, mid-17th
century

Attributed to Cornelius
Johnson, *Portrait of a
youth*, c.1650

British School, *James V
of Scotland*, c.1540

French School, *Rosa,
Consort of Suleiman,
Emperor of the Turks*,
17th century

French School, *Queen
Marconese, Consort of
Clothaire IV, King of
France*, 17th century

After Polidoro da
Caravaggio, *A nymph,
satyrs and putti*, mid-
17th century

British School,
Elizabeth Woodville,
16th century

British School, *Edward
III*, 17th century

Furniture

A 17th-century Flemish
cabinet veneered in red
tortoiseshell with silver
and silver-gilt mounts,
on a 19th-century
stand, inscribed as
having belonged to
Mary, Queen of Scots

Oak draw-leaf table in
16th-century style,
19th century

Stumpwork box,
17th century, with
embroidery of *The
Dream of Jacob*.
Associated with Mary,
Queen of Scots

Bed-hangings of
crewel-work, late
17th century, on
modern frame

Two late 17th-century
chairs or 'backstools',
with original Turkey work
covers

An Italian carved wooden
cassone or dower chest

Tapestries

Four Flemish (Antwerp)
panels from *The
History of Phaeton*
series, mid- to late
17th century:
*Apollo and Phaeton;
The fall of Phaeton;
The sisters of Phaeton;
Clymene and Phaeton*

Mary, Queen of Scots' Supper Room

Pictures

After Polidoro da
Caravaggio, *Cupids
with swans*, mid-17th
century

Follower of Paolo
Veronese, *The
Annunciation*, c.1580

Paolo Veronese, *David
victorious over Goliath*,
c.1568

After Polidoro da
Caravaggio, *Cupids
playing croquet*, mid-
17th century

British School, *'Fair
Rosamund'*, c.1720

After Polidoro da
Caravaggio, *Cupids
pulling in a net*, mid-
17th century

British School, *Portrait
of a woman*, c.1620

Paolo Veronese, *Judith
with the head of
Holofernes*, 1565

Tapestries

Flemish *verdure* or
forest panels, late 17th
century

THE MURDER OF DAVID RIZZIO

On the night of 9 March 1566 David Rizzio, Mary, Queen of Scots' Italian secretary, was brutally murdered in the Queen's Apartments at Holyroodhouse. The murderers were led by Henry, Lord Darnley, the Queen's second husband, who was violently jealous of Rizzio's influence over Mary. At the time, Mary was pregnant with their only child, the future James VI and I. Darnley led the conspirators up the private staircase to the Queen's Bedchamber from his apartment on the floor below. He rushed in upon the Queen, her ladies and Rizzio, who were in the tiny supper room, off the bedchamber. Despite clinging to the Queen's skirts, Rizzio was dragged to the adjoining Outer Chamber, stabbed 56 times and left to die.

Less than a year after Rizzio's murder, Darnley himself was also dead. He was found strangled following an explosion at Kirk O'Fields, the house where he was staying in Edinburgh. Mary then married James Hepburn, Earl of Bothwell, the main suspect in Darnley's murder, at Holyroodhouse on 15 May 1567. The marriage was universally condemned and on 14 July Mary was forced to abdicate in favour of her infant son.

*Portrait of a man, known as 'David Rizzio',
17th century.*

THE PRESENTATION OF MARY, QUEEN OF SCOTS' CHAMBERS

By the mid-18th century, the attention of visitors to the palace focused on the rooms of Mary, Queen of Scots. Their gloomy spiral staircases, thick walls and heraldic ceilings, combined with details of Mary's tragic life and the story of Rizzio's murder, exerted a powerful appeal. The Duke of Hamilton's housekeeper, who took on the duty of showing visitors these rooms, and the guidebooks of the time, claimed that the apartments had remained untouched since Mary's day and were complete with their original furniture and the floor stained with the blood of Rizzio. As early as 1760 the future Duchess of Northumberland recorded in her diary: 'I went also to see Mary Queen of Scots' Bedchamber (a very small one it is) from whence David Rizzio was drag'd out and stab'd in the ante room where is some of his Blood which they can't get wash'd out.' Many of the Duke of Hamilton's unwanted items of furniture had been placed in the second-floor rooms and these pieces gradually came to be passed off to visitors as Mary, Queen of Scots' own possessions.

Both George IV and Queen Victoria wanted to preserve these apartments with little change, but by the early 20th century this exaggerated decay had begun to look like neglect. Scholarship had improved and visitors began to question the authenticity of what they were shown. Through a succession of repairs much of the romantic visual appeal was lost, and in the mid-1970s the decision was taken to strip the rooms back to their essentials and to move the baroque furnishings to the King's Apartments on the first floor.

ABOVE: *S. D. Swarbreck*, Mary, Queen of Scots' bedchamber, *1861. The State Bed, now on display in the King's Bedchamber, can be seen clearly.*

BELOW: *An early twentieth-century photograph of Mary, Queen of Scots' Outer Chamber.*

Mary, Queen of Scots' Outer Chamber

THIS IS THE ROOM where Mary received visitors and where her
formidable encounters took place with the intractable Scottish
Protestant cleric, John Knox. The compartmented oak ceiling,
restored in the early 20th century, records in its heraldry
James V and Mary of Guise, Mary, Queen of Scots and her first
husband, the future Francis II, and his father, Henry II, King of
France. At the east end of the room is Mary's oratory. The
ceiling panel of the small oratory recess is decorated with the
Cross of St Andrew encircled by a royal crown. In Mary, Queen
of Scots' time, a window in this recess looked directly down on
the west entrance of the Abbey Church.

Mary, Queen of Scots' Chambers have been re-presented to
enhance the powerful and romantic mood for which they have
long been famous. The Outer Chamber is now devoted to a
display of Stuart and Jacobite relics. The collection consists of
treasures associated with Mary, including the Darnley Jewel, as
well as relics of the later Stuarts, such as the silver-gilt caddinet
made in Rome for Cardinal York, the brother of Prince Charles
Edward Stuart.

Pictures
(from left to right)

Alexander Fraser, *Mary,
Queen of Scots'
bedroom,
Holyroodhouse*, c.1884

Niccolò dell'Abbate,
*Portrait of a young
man with a cleft chin*,
c.1540

After Paul van Somer,
James VI and I, c.1620

Manner of Remigius
van Leemput, *Portrait
of a woman*, c.1645

British School, *Mary,
Queen of Scots*, 18th
century

Follower of Francesco
Salviati, *Giovanni della
Casa*, c.1550

British School, *'Mr
George'*, 1617

Workshop of Bernard
van Orley, *Isabella of
Austria*, c.1520

Attributed to Hans
Eworth, *Henry Stuart,
Lord Darnley and his
brother Charles, 5th
Earl of Lennox*, c.1562

British School, *Anne of
Denmark*, 17th century

German School,
*Portrait of a young
man in black*, 16th
century

British School,
Catherine of Aragon,
16th century

Flemish School, *Maria,
Queen of Hungary*,
16th century

British School, *Anne
Boleyn*, 16th century

EMBROIDERY BY MARY, QUEEN OF SCOTS

When Mary, Queen of Scots escaped from Scotland in 1568, she fled to England to seek help from her cousin, Queen Elizabeth I. Instead, the English Queen put her in the custody of George, Earl of Shrewsbury. From this time until her death in 1587, Mary, a skilled needlewoman, created many embroideries. She worked initially with Shrewsbury's wife, Elizabeth (Bess of Hardwick), discussing the designs for small panels of canvas, worked in cross stitch with coloured silks on a rectangular frame.

The figure of the cat in this panel is taken from a woodcut illustration in *Icones Animalium* by Conrad Gesner, a book on natural history published in Zurich in 1555. It is possible that the Queen was alluding to herself as the mouse and Queen Elizabeth as the cat.

THE STUART COLLECTION

Mary, Queen of Scots' Outer Chamber is devoted to a display of Stuart and Jacobite relics collected by or presented to successive sovereigns. Many pieces were acquired by Queen Mary, consort of King George V, who took a great interest in objects of family history, sorting and classifying them by type. The Stuart Collection was moved to Holyroodhouse from Windsor Castle in 1995 and is now displayed in cabinets designed by Alec Cobbe, which draw on the early seventeenth-century Scottish fashion for extravagant funerary monuments. The handwritten labels conform to the antiquarian atmosphere of the displays.

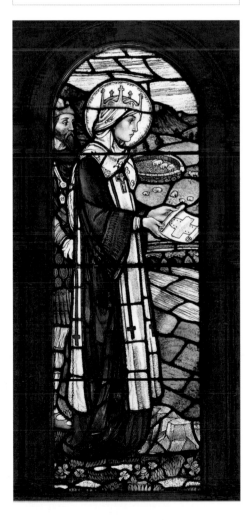

Attributed to Pieter van Coninxloo, *Portrait of a lady, possibly Jeanne de Beersel, Countess of Zollern*, c.1510–15

After Titian, *Philip II, King of Spain*, c.1620

After Anthonis Mor, *Mary I*, c.1600

British School, *Henry IV*, 17th century

British School, *Portrait of a woman*, 16th century

Attributed to Cornelius Ketel, *Portrait of a young man aged 23*, c.1600–50

After Hans Holbein the Younger, *Henry VIII*, c.1600

After William Scrots, *Edward VI*, c.1600

British School, *Don Carlos*, 16th century

British School, *Portrait of a man, known as David Rizzio*, 17th century

British School, *Portrait of a woman*, 1600-1630

Follower of Jacopo Bassano, *A mysterious appearance of a female saint*, c.1560

Ippolito Scarsellino, *The Tribute Money*, c.1615

Style of Adriaen van der Werff, *Adam and Eve*, c.1700

After Raphael, *The Holy Family with St John*, c.1660

North Italian School, *Head of Christ*, c.1525

Follower of Giovanni Bellini, *Head of a woman*, c.1510

Livinus de Vogelaare, *The Memorial of Lord Darnley*, c.1567

Tapestries

Five Flemish *verdure* or forest panels, late 17th century

Stained glass window

Louis Davis, *St Margaret*, 1927

Works of art

The works of art in the display cabinets are from the Stuart Collection and are individually labelled

RIGHT: *Stained glass window of St Margaret by Louis Davis, 1927.*

THE DARNLEY JEWEL

This spectacular jewel, intended to be worn at the neck or on the breast, was probably made for Lady Margaret Douglas, Countess of Lennox (1515–78), following the death of her husband Matthew, Earl of Lennox, Regent of Scotland in 1571. Margaret, the mother of Lord Darnley, the second husband of Mary, Queen of Scots, was the granddaughter of Henry VII of England and first cousin of Queen Elizabeth I.

The heart-shaped jewel is made from gold and richly ornamented with enamels, rubies, an emerald and a false sapphire. It is elaborately decorated on the cover, the reverse and the interior with many emblems and inscriptions, while compartments conceal further emblematic devices. These allude to the turbulent history of the Lennox family and probably also refer to Lady Margaret's hopes and ambitions for her grandson, James, son of Mary and Lord Darnley, who later became James VI and I.

The jewel was purchased by Queen Victoria in 1842 from the collection of the antiquarian Horace Walpole.

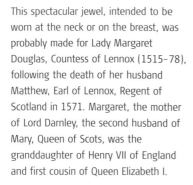

LEFT: *Attributed to Hans Eworth,* Henry, Lord Darnley and his brother Charles, 5th Earl of Lennox. *c.1562*

RIGHT: *François Clouet,* Mary, Queen of Scots in white mourning, *c.1558–61*

BELOW: *Livinus de Vogelaare,* The Memorial to Lord Darnley, *c.1567*

The Abbey Church and Gardens

BUILDING OF THE ABBEY CHURCH probably began shortly after its foundation in 1128 by David I for the Augustinian Canons. Only a processional door leading from the cloisters survives from this period, visible from the gardens on the south wall. This simple first church was to prove too small for the requirements of the community and a new building programme was begun *c.*1195 and continued until *c.*1230, to provide a much larger and more ambitious structure. This was constructed around the original church, to allow for continued use until most of the new church was in place, when the older building was demolished.

The north wall of the nave was probably the first area to be built. The earliest part is decorated with distinctive interlaced arcading with waterleaf capitals. As work advanced, the style changed and the aisle windows are of pointed form with stiff leaf capitals. The south wall and aisle was originally of three storeys. The high central space of the nave was covered with a stone vault, but only a small area survives. The impressive west front, with its richly ornamented and recessed doorway, faced Edinburgh, and extra width was created with two square towers which extended beyond the walls of the nave. The south tower was eventually absorbed into the palace, but the north tower survives to dominate the view down the Canongate. Extensive monastic buildings were added to accommodate the large community, including cloisters, a chapter house, a refectory and monastic and royal guest houses.

ROYAL BURIALS

The Abbey Church of Holyrood was the site of many royal burials over the years. James II (1437–60) was buried within its precincts, as were David II (1329–71), James V (1513–42) and his first wife, Madeleine of Valois (d.1537), and Henry, Lord Darnley (1545–67), second husband of Mary, Queen of Scots. After the Reformation and later destructive raids, the vaults were violated and the various monuments destroyed. The royal remains were later collected together and interred in the Royal Vault in the south-eastern corner of the church, surrounded by many handsome monuments.

TOP: *The interior of the Abbey Church.*

BELOW: *The Abbey Church from the gardens.*

BELOW: *The south aisle and vault.*

ABOVE: *David Roberts,* Ruins of the Abbey of Holyrood, *1823.*

The abbey was completed *c.*1250, but the stone vault caused problems from an early date and, in the fifteenth century, Abbot Crawford added two levels of flying buttresses for support.

The abbey suffered badly from the destructive raids from English armies, particularly the Rough Wooing raid of 1544. At this time the brass eagle lectern of the abbey, a gift from Abbot George Crichton, was looted by Sir Richard Lee and later presented by him to St Stephen's Parish Church in St Alban's, Hertfordshire. The abbey's monastic buildings were abandoned after the Reformation and in 1570 the eastern parts of the church, ruined as a result of the earlier attacks, were finally demolished. The nave was the only part retained for use, adopted as the parish church for the burgh of Canongate.

Changes were made to the abbey for the Scottish coronation of Charles I in 1633, when the east end was remodelled to include a large tracery window and the west front was amended and embellished. The abbey underwent additional changes when, during the reign of James VII and II, it was refitted for Catholic worship, as the Chapel Royal and the chapel for Knights of the Order of the Thistle. Further damage was done when, in 1688, the abbey was ransacked by the Edinburgh mob.

BELOW: *The west front of the abbey at night.*

The instability of the abbey was finally to prove insurmountable when, after further repairs, the roof collapsed in 1768. During the 19th century, the picturesque remains added to the romantic setting of the palace and the historical presentation of the drama of the life of Mary, Queen of Scots. The scenic ruin attracted and inspired artists and writers; in 1829 the composer Felix Mendelssohn visited Edinburgh and was moved by the melancholy grandeur of the abbey to write his Scottish symphony.

In 1910–11, the site of the transepts and choir was excavated by the Office of Works and the foundations left exposed in the garden, to allow the extent of the Abbey Church and its accompanying buildings to be visualised. Excavations in 2006 revealed walls and floors of some of the early monastic buildings.

The ten-acre palace gardens are encircled by the Queen's Park and form a contrasting foreground to the spectacular natural landscape beyond.

Until the time of James IV the gardens were primarily under monastic control. The marshy ground was drained and the surrounding area enclosed within a wall and cultivated for monastic use. Further activity coincided with the development of the palace buildings and the royal marriages of James IV and James V. By the time Mary, Queen of Scots was resident at the palace there was a series of enclosed gardens, including a walled Privy Garden to the north, and areas for cultivation and recreation. Jousting and archery took place within the grounds and there was a tennis court to the west of the palace. Further works were undertaken at the time of James VI's visit in 1617 and for Charles I's Scottish coronation in 1633.

The two surviving relics of this early garden are 'Queen Mary's Bath', probably a 16th-century garden building, to the north-west, and a faceted sundial, designed and carved by John Mylne in 1633, which can now be seen in the North Garden.

TOP: *The gardens from the East.*

ABOVE: *The Royal Company of Archers shooting in the gardens.*

LEFT. *Neil Oliver inspects a trench in the palace gardens during Channel 4 Time Team's 'Big Royal Dig' in 2006.*

LEFT: *'Queen Mary's sundial'.*

LEFT: *View from the roof of the palace looking south-west to Salisbury Crags.*

BELOW: *Schoolgirls dancing in the grounds of Holyroodhouse, 14 July 1934.*

During the 1670s a Privy Garden was planned to the east, to be overlooked by the new Royal Apartments. In the early 18th century these gardens were still flourishing. Daniel Defoe described them in *A Tour Through the Whole Island of Great Britain* of 1724: 'one is like our apothecaries' garden at Chelsea, called a physic garden, and is tolerably well stored with simples, and some exotics of value; and, particularly I was told, there was a rhubarb tree, or plant, and which throve very well.'

By the time Queen Victoria and her family stayed at the palace, the gardens were overgrown and the lower end of the Royal Mile consisted of slums and industrial buildings. Prince Albert took a close interest in the redevelopment of the palace's immediate surroundings. A new carriage approach was made to the north, avoiding the not very salubrious Canongate, but in the process the Privy Garden was swept away. New planting areas were created to the north and south of the palace. To the east, the garden wall provided the same effect as an original 18th-century ha-ha, or hidden ditch, concealing the actual boundary of the garden to give the impression that it flowed naturally into the park beyond. Screens of trees were planted to hide the nearby breweries and gasworks. During the reign of George V and Queen Mary the gardens continued to be improved and were laid out with herbaceous borders and a long rockery.

Today the gardens provide the setting for The Queen's garden parties, held annually in July for around 8,000 people.